## Hamed Ekhtiari, MD, PhD

Hamed Ekhtiari, MD, Ph.D., is a faculty member at the Laureate Institute for Brain Research (LIBR), Tulsa, OK, USA. His lab is focused on reshaping the future of psychiatry and addiction medicine using cognitive training in combination with brain imaging and non-invasive brain stimulation technologies. Dr. Ekhtiari has published numerous peer-reviewed articles and book chapters and has presented in many international meetings. As a neuroscientist and internationally known expert in addiction neuroscience, Dr. Ekhtiari has developed and tested novel cognitive training programs for behavior change, including Neurocognitive Empowerment for Addiction Treatment (NEAT). Dr. Ekhtiari also directs the Brain Awareness for Recovery Initiative (BARI). BARI incorporates neuroscience content, with cartoons and affiliated text in neurocognitive informed psychoeducation and training, targeting different cognitive mechanisms associated with recovery. BARI materials are translated and culturally adopted by scientific authorities in 18 languages in 5 continents so far. He has also studied the underlying neural mechanisms of response to food and drug-related cues using fMRI and is currently translating these findings into clinical use.

## Meghedi Vartanian, M.Sc

Meghedi Vartanian, M.Sc., is a clinical psychologist who has received her B.Sc. and M.Sc. from University of Tehran within the quota for exceptional talents. As a professionally trained psychologist, she has spent her academic career reading and writing the overeating causes and consequences which gives her a unique voice that shines through her new path of discovering this world by conducting new studies. Besides her academic activities, she has been involved clinically by holding group therapy sessions, helping people to raise their awareness about the brain and its function in their daily life to have a healthy body.

# Content

Introduction / **6**

How to read this book / **12**

 Step1: **Determining Goals and Motivations** / **15**

Step2: **My Brain's Journey Toward Change** / **25**

 Step3: **Food Craving vs. Hunger** / **37**

Step4: **Triggers and Craving Response** / **45**

 Step5: **Food Cues in Our Environment that Makes Us Eat More and More** / **53**

Step6: **Environmental Engineering** / **61**

 Step7: **Emotional Triggers** / **69**

Step8: **Eating for Emotion Regulation** / **79**

 Step9: **Emotion Regulation for Eating Management** / **87**

Step10: **Behavioral Activation and Self-Entertainment Skills** / **95**

 Step11: **Social Values and Eating Behavior** / **103**

Step12: **Peer Pressure and Eating** / **111**

Step13: **When Prevention is more Effective than Self-Control / 119**

Step14: **Craving Inhibition / 129**

Step15: **Craving Reappraisal / 141**

Step16: **Relationship Engineering / 151**

Step17: **Destructive Thoughts and Behaviors / 161**

Step18: **Amplifying Inhibitory Control / 169**

Step19: **Habitual Eating and Eating Habits / 177**

Step20: **Supporting Activities for Recovery / 185**

Step21: **Automatic Eating / 193**

Step22: **Mindfulness, Emotions and Eating / 203**

Step23: **Lapse and Relapse Preventiong / 211**

Step24: **Conscious Eating and Mindful Emotions / 219**

Summary in ten steps / **229**

# Introduction

**If you have only 15 minutes**

If you want to review the main message of this book in just fifteen minutes, we will offer you the following ten key points.

**❶ The crucial role of "weight loss" is undeniable throughout your life quality. Take it seriously!**

Have you ever encountered someone who is paralyzed by a stroke? Have you been in contact with people who have a disability due to myocardial infarction? Nearly 50 percent of us, if we do not lose our lives due to sudden accidents, we will suffer from a severe disability due to stroke and heart attacks or death comes to us by them. Reducing only 5-10% of your weight reduces the likelihood of heart attacks and strokes by up to 50%. If you can add 30 minutes of daily exercise to this weight loss, the probability is down to a quarter. Why do we have to let our brain and heart arteries get stuck and tear? For instance, in case of stroke, we go to the angiography and get a stent and heart bypass surgery to survive, when the best surgeons, even by receiving thousands of dollars, can't do anything to cure the problem?

**❷ "Not eating and dieting" are not ways of losing weight; your brain functions should be changed!**

Perhaps you have seen among your friends, or you yourself have experienced keeping diet for months, although it does reduce the weight somewhat, after a while this weight is regained and sometimes even to a greater extent. Research in recent years has shown that diet and nutrition deprivation are not a weight loss solution. A weight loss solution is a "change in your cognition". But what is "cognition"? Cognition refers to the set of processes performed in your brain and "cognitive neuroscience" is the knowledge that examines these processes in your brain. The findings of cognitive science over the last few years provide us with methods that can be used to change the individual's "cognition". Changing cognition and its subsequent behavior about eating is the ultimate solution to the overweight problem. In this book, we will look at ways of changing brain functions and cognition.

**③ Your craving to eat, without being hungry, is one of the main causes of your overweight.**

The brain of many overweight people is very sensitive to all the triggers associated with eating, such as the smell of delicious food, colorful showcase filled with sweets, maple-roasted bacon, turning a cooking magazine page, and even thinking about memories of eating a delicious meal in a famous restaurant. All these triggers make them crave. Resisting against this feeling of tenderness and craving, although may be effective for a few minutes, ultimately results in uncontrolled eating. In people who are overweight, modifying brain activities is critical to success in weight loss. This modification of activity will be possible by changing attitudes and exercises during the cognitive and behavioral rectification sessions.

**④ Do not let your body and brain getting greedy for foods.**

Food deprivation in the form of intensive diets, without the use of cognitive interventions, makes your body and brain greedy. Many people, who have experienced common diets in the society, after a short period of weight loss, find themselves even more obese than before. What is the point? Deprivation of food and long-term hunger leads to changes in your body that prepare it for the absorption of more foods. For example, it increases the intestinal villi and also stimulates your body's fat tissues to absorb and store the ingested food as much as possible. Food deprivation periods in the form of diets change your brain in a way that makes it more sensitive to food triggers. In this situation, seeing a small chocolate chip cookie may melt your heart, and if you face a box of them, maybe it leads to uncontrolled eating in a short time. But what is the solution? How can we prevent the food-oriented greediness of the brain and the body, despite the fact of losing weight? Cognitive interventions by changing attitudes and modifying the way you change your brain and body during food deprivation, while you're losing weight, create conditions that your brain and your body, will lose their desire for food without being greedy. In this book, we will cover these cognitive interventions during the 24 steps.

**⑤ Eating as a tool for regulating negative feelings and emotions is one of the main reasons for being overweight.**

Eating favorite foods can be a good way to reduce negative feelings and emotions such as sadness, anxiety, anger, embarrassment, or hatred. In that way, you eat to regulate emotions. But people who use eating as an emotion regulator are in the risk of being overweight. There are other more effective ways to regulate emotions that we do not know or do not have the skill to use. If you are one of those people who "eat" to regulate the emotions and also want to lose weight, you should use other effective ways to manage and regulate your emotions and feelings, so that, with time passing, you will see the tremendous effect of "changing cognition" in your weight.

**⑥ Environmental engineering is one of the most important ways to reduce weight.**

Trying to control the craving after encountering a very appetizing sweet, or trying not to eat when sitting around a big dinner table with a group of friends, or not using sausages in the refrigerator when you arrive home hungry is very difficult. A more effective solution is to prevent craving by modifying the environment and interpersonal relationships. Having skill in environmental engineering, to prevent craving is a must for the success of a weight loss program. But changing the behavior and modifying the environment is not as easy as it sounds. Any change in behavior should be gradual and after a serious change in your attitude.

**⑦ Eating with feelings of guilt and shame is one of the serious factors in your obesity.**

As mentioned, many overweight people tend to eat more when they are upset and sad, as an attempt to improve their mood by eating. When upset or sad, cravings will start slightly, but increase quickly. In many cases, they feel guilty after eating. This happens regularly in people who want to lose their weight, and this feeling of guilt leads to more negative feelings. This negative feeling multiplies a person's craving, and the overeating will lead to more weight gain. In other words, the person enters into a vicious cycle of craving and negative mood. This cycle (i.e. negative feeling ⟶ eating ⟶ negative feeling ⟶ eating..........) is one of the major challenges faced by overweight people. It should be noted that the increasing need for eating and craving, as a result of negative mood, is a natural thing. Many people start craving due to stress or negative mood. It is important to accept that it is normal to experience cravings, but this acceptance never means giving up and accompanying this feeling. One also needs to have a commitment to finding the right behavior to deal with negative feelings and cravings and manage them.

**⑧ Changing inappropriate habits, beliefs, and rituals of eating are essential for weight loss.**

Our habits, beliefs and behaviors while eating play an important role in our weight gain. Fast, unattended and unconscious eating while doing daily things; like, studying, or watching a television program, leads to overeating and eventually being overweight. It is said that these bad habits lead to receiving hidden calories. In this situation, if we want to know how many calories we receive per day, we cannot count them, since in many cases we are not even aware of our eating, and we do not know how much we have eaten in order to calculate our caloric intake. But unfortunately, our body absorbs and uses those calories. Therefore, one of the important steps in losing weight is identifying inappropriate and unconscious eating habits, or unconscious behaviors. Unconscious, or habitual behaviors, are very fast and, in many cases, go under our radar and it's difficult to correct them. In this book, you will first learn how to recognize inappropriate and unconscious eating habits or behaviors and then correct them. Modifying bad social rituals and habits should be considered in the process of losing weight. For example: Accepting to eat more at dinner parties, placing rice/pasta or other high dense carbohydrates as an eternal part of the table, or not eliminating eating from any parties or family gatherings are signs of bad social rituals and habits that need to be modified.

### ⑨ If eating is one of the few pleasures you enjoy, being overweight is inevitable.

The human brain needs enjoyment and getting rewards, and you need to supply this as best as you can. It is possible to respond to this need by smoking, eating sweet and greasy foods, having high-risk sexual behaviors, or by finding more effective and healthier ways to meet this need. Having fun and responding to the "need for pleasure" in a healthy way is one of the arts and skills that people with overweight are weak in. With that said, just saying "Go and find another entertainment rather than eating!" is not the solution to this problem. Changing the human behavior and modifications of the previous lifestyle is not possible simply. In this book, you will be taught how to change gradually.

### ⑩ Sustained weight loss is only achieved over time and with patience and perseverance.

When you plant a small sapling in the front yard and you water it every day. Although you may not see it's growth day by day, you're sure that these small seedlings will become a young and beautiful tree, after a long time, if you continue to care. Losing weight and reaching an ideal body will occur over a period of time and it will only be decisive if you spend time and energy on the right track. You cannot see these changes day by day, but you will see the progression of it during the months. Our experience suggests that the loss of about two pounds per month during the change of cognition and behavior will be ideal. In these situations, it usually takes about one, two or three years to reach the optimal weight. Be patient and be sure of the results, this type of weight loss will be irreversible.

### If you have only 5 minutes

If you take a quick look at various advertisements in newspapers, magazines or the Internet, you will come across diverse messages to introduce different weight loss methods which can indicate two important points: First, there are many people who are overweight and are faced with the consequences of it, and secondly, the various methods are recommended for treatment.

You've been seeing these ads for years. But what's the problem? Why, although we all know, obesity is problematic, and what causes' being overweight is excessive eating, many people in the community still face this problem? And why, although they often decide to lose their weight, and test different methods, they still cannot reach the desired weight? Why are weight loss methods and dietary regimens not so effective? And why do people repeatedly fail in these ways? As you know, weight loss plays an important role in raising the quality of life for those who are overweight. If obese people can only reduce their weight by 10%, they can reduce the risk of heart attacks and stroke by 50%. This is just one of the most important effects of weight loss. But how can we lose our weight with an appropriate method? This is the most important question that every overweight person asks from professionals in this field. To answer this question, it's better to first ask why some people eat more than their own physical needs. This question is a bit deeper because it helps us to diagnose where the problem is? This question has a self-contained answer, and it is that dieting is not the only solution. Before starting a diet, there are other things to do. In fact, the problem is not eating; the problem is "Why do we eat?"! In this book, you will learn that what controls the eating process is not your empty stomach, but the function of your BRAIN. The brain has a complex function, and we cannot change its function of eating with a simple diet plan or a hard diet. If you take a closer look at your behavior, you will find that in most cases, your eating is not due to hunger, but sometimes you eat because you enjoy eating, or when you are angry you eat in order to make yourself a little calm. Even in these situations, the eagerness of eating is much more than when you are hungry. Sometimes you don't even know why you eat, you only experience a strong sense of need or urge to eat within yourself. In this case, you have a craving that may increase when you are sad or anxious. So, to lose weight, we should not just look for a diet. It's better to first identify your thoughts and behavior when eating and learn methods, such as preventing or modifying craving, changing the habits of eating, engineering your living environment and relationships and emotional regulation. With their help, our thoughts and behaviors will change and as a result, many of the behaviors that lead to overeating also change. Ultimately, the result of this change in the brain, that will be reflected in your behavior and attitude, is weight loss. That being said, changing the brain requires time. We cannot change our thoughts and behaviors suddenly. These are all the realities of weight loss, so never go for ultra-fast ways to change, because it's not possible. For a change to happen it is essential to be aware of the problem, to accept deficiencies, and to commit in a step by step modification. To meet these goals, join us in this book.

### If you have only 30 seconds

If you are struggling with being overweight, you should first answer this question before taking any action for your treatment: Are you eating just because of hunger and your body's need? If the answer is negative, then a diet that forces you not to eat will not be helpful. It's better to know first why you eat more than your body needs? You eat more often because you enjoy eating, or sometimes you eat to reduce your turmoil, and in many people, overeating has become a behavioral habit, so that if they eat less, they feel bad. Therefore, in many cases, eating is not due to the need for the body and hunger, but a way of controlling and regulating emotions and feelings. Many overweight people usually use eating to reduce their negative feelings and emotions, and they are not aware of proper emotion regulation skills. In this book, you will become familiar with how your brain makes thoughts, behaviors, and feelings about eating. By knowing your brain better you will have the skills to change your thoughts, behaviors, and emotions and ultimately achieve your ideal weight.

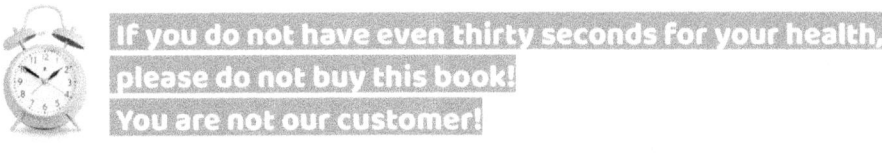

### If you do not have even thirty seconds for your health, please do not buy this book! You are not our customer!

# How to read this book

The philosophy behind this book is to provide you with educational training that will help you to reduce your weight by managing your overeating behavior. This will be achieved by creating self-awareness about how your brain processes your "relationship with food." The tutorials of this book have been presented during 24-steps/sessions. In each step, you are asked to answer a few questions or do some exercises. Accordingly, this book can be considered as an "educational and training book." We generally prefer to read a book from the beginning to the end without setting pen to paper and doing the exercises of the book. Doing exercises, thinking and actively answering and, finally, writing about personal thoughts and feelings are still unseasoned in our culture. Although our recommendation is to have a pen or pencil while studying this book and responding actively to questions, please do not push yourself too hard! Read this book any way you like, with or without pens, while sitting, standing or even sleeping! Just please read this book!

Decreasing just 10% of your weight will reduce the risk of many major diseases by half! Studies show that except for accidents, other deaths are up to 60% affected by obesity. If we want to have a long and healthy life, we must seriously think about our overweight. Although our first suggestion is to study this book, in any way you like, but for those readers who want to use this book much better, we suggest you do the following:

1. **Study the book step by step and over time:** It is recommended that this book is studied at a maximum speed of one step per day for one month and at least one step per week for six months. Although it is possible to read the book overnight or in a few days, a proper understanding of content and the effectiveness of the book requires time and practice.

2. **Doing exercises during the study of each step:** In the content of each step, there are a number of exercises to do while studying. A number of exercises are also at the end of each step to provide a better understanding of the teachings presented. We suggest you to do the ending practices of each step after studying the contents of each step and thinking

deeply about them. Even a few readers respond to these exercises after the following days and still have taken very positive outcomes from the training and practice.

3. **Record the date of each step and its exercises:** At the top left of the beginning of each step, as well as the top of the page entitled "Your own footsteps on this journey," there is a space to record the date of the study and its related exercises. It is suggested that you register the date of each step so that you can follow your progress in this book.

4. **Talking about the lessons of this book and sharing them with others:** After reading the teachings of this book and thinking deeply about them, share the summary and results of these teachings with friends, family members, and people around and ask their opinions on this. See if they think like you or have any suggestions or criticisms about your thoughts. Talking about the teachings of this book will give you more power to act. Do not be embarrassed to worry about your overweight and study of this book.

5. **Applying the teachings of this book in speech, thought or behavior:** Think about the teachings of this book throughout the day. Try to correct your beliefs and ways of thinking based on these teachings and see the effect of this change on your behavior. Practicing the teachings of this book step by step will lead you to your ultimate goal, which is "having a healthy life with a proper weight".

6. **Weighing and recording it on a regular basis during the study of the book:** We do not want you to reduce your weight during the study of this book, but we only want you to weigh and register it on a regular basis. At the end of each step, there is a space for recording your weight. For example, if the studying of the first step lengthens from Sunday to Wednesday, register your weight on Sundays, Mondays, and Tuesdays in the table at the end of the first step, and record the weight of Wednesday in the table at the end of the second step. The habit of regular daily weighting, and accepting it as it is, will ultimately help you manage weight.

7. **Acceptance and commitment to change:** The key to your success in weight management is to accept the «existence of a problem» without negative feelings such as the feeling of failure or guilt, and talking about this problem with others without feeling embarrassed. After the acceptance phase, the "commitment to change" is essential to succeed in solving the problem. A sign of commitment is the readiness to pay the costs of the change path. This cost includes reading this book at the best of available times throughout the day, spending mental energy on thinking about the teachings and solving exercises completely with pleasure, and if necessary, accepting financial costs for attending relevant therapeutic sessions, or the use of expert advisors or counselors in this field. You should know that no change is made without cost, and more important and useful changes usually need more investments. The most important cost to succeed on this path is to determine the appropriate time for studying this book and do its suggestions at the beginning of your daily tasks.

It is hoped that performing the above seven recommendations will help you make the most of this book. This book is a good start for weight loss, but it does not necessarily provide all the needs of the audience. Sometimes it is necessary to move forward on the pathway of change by getting help from a coach, a counselor, teacher or supervisor. Fortunately, in recent years, expert counselors have been trained on the basis of the scientific documentation of this book and are prepared to be alongside you, if needed. But keep in mind that reading this book alone is a huge step in your journey for change. We hope this change will bring you a whole host of happiness and health for the future.

Step 1    Date: ...... / ...... / ......

# Determining Goals and Motivations

**Why do you want to lose weight?** (goals, reasons, consequences, and motivations)

When approaching the idea of weight loss, you need to ask yourself a fundamental question, *"What is my reason for wanting to lose weight?"* To answer this basic question, you should review your reasons for managing your weight and eating habits.

✎ **What are your reasons for losing weight? Which of the following examples may be a reason for your weight loss?**
1. Because I want to go to my son's school with peace of mind, and without embarrassment, to speak with his teachers.
2. Because I'm tired of backaches and sore feet.
3. Because I cannot find a suitable job due to my weight.
4. Because I want to participate in activities such as hiking, jogging or even bungee jumping, which is not possible with this weight.
5.

Your responses to the above question may include the following: "I want to be more attractive", "I want to be praised by others", "I want to feel better physically", and so on. By reviewing your reasons for losing weight, you will find that some of them arise from an inner need: "I'll be in a better mood," while some of them arise from outwardly-focused needs such as, "People will admire me" or "People will pay more attention to me".

Each of your reasons for losing weight creates mental energy, and this energy will give you the determination to both start and continue your journey toward good health. We call this energy, "motivation". Motivation influences our thinking and behavior to help us to move forward.

It is common to have desires and wishes, but simply having a wish is not enough to propel you toward a goal. What makes you move forward to reach your desires is the motivation derived from your reasons for achieving what you desire. Motivation is the energy that propels you on the journey towards your goal. Motivations, as well as reasons, are divided into two categories: internal (intrinsic) and external (extrinsic). An intrinsic motivator is an inner force that propels you to do something. In contrast, an extrinsic motivator is an outer force that propels you to do something. If you decide to lose weight in order to experience inner well-being and health, your motivation is intrinsic, and if you decide to lose weight in order to receive praise and encouragement from others, your motivation is extrinsic. It does not matter whether your motivations are intrinsic or extrinsic, but it is important to strengthen your motivations and keep them in front of you, like a carrot on a stick, so you can stay focused on your journey toward good health.

❝ **Now look back at your reasons for losing weight and determine the degree of motivation associated with each reason. Score the motivation of each reason from 0-10, with 0 being not at all motivating to 10, being extremely motivating.** ❞

Another important issue to address, on this first step of your journey, is the goals and consequences that you have in mind when reading this book and completing its training. Many readers define their **goal** in this way: "I want to lose X lbs. (kg)". For example, "I want to lose 50 pounds (20 kilograms) by the end of this program, and achieving this goal would make me happy." Most likely, your main goal is to lose weight, but the training in this book can easily be applied to other goals. Another goal might be the following: "My goal is to be healthy. I want to learn skills that will help me to have a healthy lifestyle. I want to lose weight and maintain a healthy weight." Because you can control your weight with the skills in this book and achieve your desired weight goals, the preceding goal of losing weight is more achievable and more effective. Therefore, it is important to choose realistic goals at the beginning of your journey toward good health.

**Other than "weight loss", what are your main goals related to this book and its training? Others have answered this question this way:**
1. I want to improve my brain functions.
2. I want to regain my health.
3. I want to prove to myself that I can solve my problems.
4. I want to know more about myself and have better self-awareness.
5. 

So far, you have learned that to achieve any goal, including weight loss, you must consciously specify your reasons for beginning the change. By identifying and exploring these reasons, you will gain a sustainable level of motivation that will accompany you to the end of your journey. You have also learned that it is better to have a realistic view of your goal because achieving each goal will have (positive or negative) consequences. Predicting those consequences and their effects on your life also helps you to have a realistic view of your goals. Please answer the following exercises completely, writing down your answers. Doing the exercises is important because by doing so; you will come to a better understanding of yourself. In fact, what helps you to lose weight is not just "not eating," **it's also a change in your way of thinking and a change in your behavior, at each moment of your life**. However, for every change, we must first know what we want to change. Doing these exercises will help you to create a deep awareness of how you think and behave.

We know that thinking may be a difficult task, especially when you are trying to think about your thoughts, feelings, desires, demands, and behaviors, but we want you to talk and write about yourself because it will help you to lose weight. It is important that you acquire all the skills that will help you on your journey toward good health. So, try to read the book carefully and think about its teachings. If there are any parts you do not understand, ask for help from your peers and friends.

**Mark ☑ the items that relate to you. Draw a table, like the following for yourself and write down the consequence of the goal of losing weight or maintaining your current weight.**

Consequences of maintaining my current weight:

| Positive consequence | Negative consequence |
|---|---|
| I can continue eating ☐ | The likelihood of having a stroke increases ☐ |
| I do not have to exercise every day ☐ | I will lose my attraction ☐ |
| I don't have to prepare food separately from family members ☐ | I cannot wear my favorite dress ☐ |
| I can show that I have accepted my current weight and I'm confident about it ☐ | My knee pain gets worse ☐ |
| I can buy my favorite sweets ☐ | My relatives think of me as an idle person ☐ |
| I can enjoy the pleasures of eating ☐ | I cannot go to the pool easily ☐ |
| I can make myself happy with eating whenever I'm upset ☐ | My family is so embarrassed that I'm too fat ☐ |
| I can cook any food I want ☐ | I cannot have the convenience of mobility ☐ |

### Consequences of reducing my current weight

| Positive consequence | Negative consequence |
|---|---|
| I will be light and healthy ☐ | Dining out is my biggest fan, I'll miss it ☐ |
| I will look more attractive ☐ | I cannot eat whatever I want ☐ |
| I can go more confidently to the pool ☐ | I will miss some gatherings ☐ |
| I can wear my favorite dress ☐ | I should always be under the pressure of the diet ☐ |
| I can easily attend parties ☐ | I get nervous ☐ |
| My confidence will increase ☐ | I have to make special foods for myself ☐ |
| I would love myself more ☐ | I cannot make myself happy by eating ☐ |
| My family will be proud of me ☐ | I will watch my favorite foods wistfully ☐ |

Brain Box
## What's going on in your brain?

Before reading this section, think about the following questions:

- Can a conversation about complications of obesity, make a person more motivated to lose weight?
- Does the human brain get more incentive to change its behavior by getting more information?

Let's start our discussion with cigarette advertising. As you have already seen, there are many, often annoying, pictures and warnings on cigarette packs like what you see here. The impact of these images on smoking has always been the main concern: Have these images actually been successful in reducing the smoking rate? Or have they had the opposite effect, contrary to expectations, and increased smoking?

The studies showed different results in the two groups of smokers and non-smokers. After seeing the advertisement smoking actually increased among smokers, while non-smokers were less likely to smoke. What is the reason behind this?

When we label people and point out their risky behaviors, those who don't participate continue to abstain, but those who are at the root of the problem will dig themselves deeper, perhaps thinking, "black will take no other hue! It's my body and I love to smoke, it's not your business, in the end, we all die anymore, nobody has eternal life!" to try to calm themselves down, but with these self-soothing statements, they fall into a swamp from which they cannot easily escape.

**But how does this issue relate to obesity or being overweight?**

Maybe you have experienced this yourself. For example, a person with diabetes who constantly hears that he should not eat sweets, or that he could lose his vision or a limb. Despite these cautions, he may start eating more sweets, or furtively eating his favorite cake, when no one is watching.

Continuing to remind people that they are obese, and warning them of related problems such as stroke, brain pressure, cataracts, heart and lung problems, pancreatitis, diabetes, fatty liver, gallstones, blood pressure, back pain, women's problems, cancer, skin problems, varicose veins, etc., is not helpful, and the stress and discomfort caused by these constant warnings can exacerbate the cravings and unhealthy habits for overweight people. Managing overeating in people who have serious complications such as diabetes, history of heart attack, or joint erosion can be more difficult than when dealing with individuals without these complications. So, knowing that losing weight is good for health does not always help us, instead stigma related to obesity damages people's confidence. In order to reduce their emotional distress, they tell themselves, "Inside, I'm still just me, I ain't no looker, it's not only the length of life that does matter but the way you live it," so that their life is not further complicated. Understanding the side effects of obesity not only does not help change, but it also creates more stress, causing people to avoid help rather than seek out help. This is the primary failure of unsuccessful treatments, but it can act as a preventive measure for people who are in the margins of obesity. You will read in the next steps how happiness is an effective factor to increase your brain's ability to manage overeating.

Date: ...... / ...... / ......

# Your Own Footsteps on this Journey...

**1** **Please read the reasons listed in the table below and determine the level of motivation derived from each of them by writing a number, from 0 (unimportant) to 10 (extremely important). At the bottom of the table, add other reasons and determine how much you are motivated by them.**

| Reasons for losing weight | Motivation (0 to 10) |
|---|---|
| If I lose weight, I will look more attractive. | |
| If I lose weight, others will admire me. | |
| If I lose weight, I will not worry about diseases like diabetes or high blood pressure. | |
| If I lose weight, I will be more willing to go to the pool. | |
| If I lose weight, I will feel better when dancing in public. | |
| If I lose weight, the feeling of pressure on my chest and the pain in my heart will be reduced. | |
| If I lose weight, I will feel better eating in public. | |
| If I lose weight, I will feel better physically. | |
| If I lose weight, my confidence will increase. | |
| If I lose weight, I will be able to choose fashionable clothes. | |
| If I lose weight, I will feel better about myself and criticize myself less. | |
| If I lose weight, I will think I've done a good job and I will feel determined about making more changes. | |
| If I lose weight, I will be able to move around easier. | |
| If I lose weight, I will avoid heart attack and stroke. | |

**2** Make a list of your most important reasons and write it on a paper or card. Carry it with you, or place it somewhere (on the refrigerator, for example), so you can read it every day.

**3** In your opinion, what problems or obstacles do you think may reduce your motivation on your health journey? Write down at least four of these problems or obstacles in the space below. How do you think you can mitigate these problems or overcome these obstacles?

.................................................................................................................................
.................................................................................................................................
.................................................................................................................................
.................................................................................................................................
.................................................................................................................................
.................................................................................................................................
.................................................................................................................................
.................................................................................................................................
.................................................................................................................................

**4** Write down your summary of the exercises in this step. What goals, reasons, and consequences give you the most motivation to stay on this journey and continue this course?

.................................................................................................................................
.................................................................................................................................
.................................................................................................................................
.................................................................................................................................
.................................................................................................................................
.................................................................................................................................
.................................................................................................................................
.................................................................................................................................
.................................................................................................................................
.................................................................................................................................

## Health Note

- If you lose 10 percent of your current weight, your risk of heart attack and stroke will be reduced by half. Adding 30 minutes of exercise each day further reduces this to quarter. There isn't any medicine or other intervention in the health sector that has such an amazing effect on your life.

- Daily, regular weighing, at a fixed time and recorded on a form, is one of the most important factors in losing weight. To do this effectively, you need to have a high-precision, accurate, digital scale and put it in a fixed place, where you will use it regularly. Having a good scale is essential for success, so invest in one for the sake of your health. However, be careful: Right now your purpose for weighing yourself is not for daily weight loss; you simply need to pay attention to your weight and how it varies from day to day. Try to (1) accept your weight without being judgmental about it, and (2) become comfortable and accepting with your weight as it is.

| Day | Monday | Tuesday | Wednesday | Thursday | Friday | Saturday | Sunday |
|---|---|---|---|---|---|---|---|
| | / / | / / | / / | / / | / / | / / | / / |
| Weight | | | | | | | |

**Daily Weight Table**

## Summary

1 We will start our journey for change by identifying our goals, but, over time, we hope to transform our goals into our values. Goals are achieved over time, but values drive long term behavior, perhaps, throughout our entire lifetime. Achieving a certain degree of weight loss is a great goal, but we hope to transform the goal of weight loss into the value of "investing time and effort in a healthy lifestyle". This personal value can last forever. We will discuss the issue of values in greater detail throughout the book.

Now you have your goals, the reasons for achieving those goals, and the consequences and rewards of achieving them. These factors and how they relate to one another will energize you to achieve your goals. Becoming aware of these factors, and writing them down in this book will help you to begin and maintain the process of change.

**2** Many people who "would like to lose weight" are not aware of goals, reasons, and consequences and therefore, do not have sufficient motivation to start or continue on the process of change.

**3** Achieving any goal, including weight loss or health promotion, will have its own positive and negative consequences. Discussing these consequences will help you find sufficient reasons and the necessary motivation to reach your important goals of life.

**4** By knowing the obstacles you may encounter along the way, you may prepare yourself to deal with them.

**5** Weight loss is an important and complicated topic. Many people do not spend enough time thinking about and setting their goals. A detailed examination of goals, reasons, and consequences gives you the energy needed to keep you on track.

**6**

## Summary Graph

In below graph, you see a goal, three sample reasons (with different levels of motivation **M** from 1-100) and consequence of reaching to the goal.

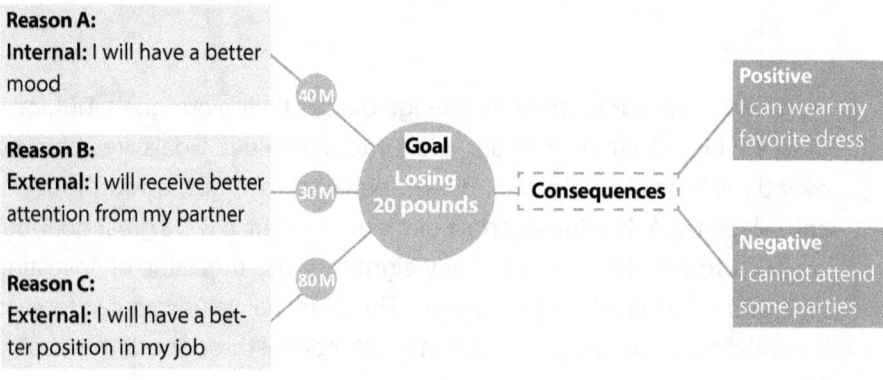

**Reason A:**
**Internal:** I will have a better mood

**Reason B:**
**External:** I will receive better attention from my partner

**Reason C:**
**External:** I will have a better position in my job

**Goal**
Losing 20 pounds

**Consequences**

**Positive**
I can wear my favorite dress

**Negative**
I cannot attend some parties

---

If you want to read more

1. Heydari, G. R., Ramezankhani, A., & Talischi, F. (2011). The impacts of cigarette packaging pictorial warning labels on smokers in the city of tehran. Tanaffos, 10(1), 40–47.
2. Ratneswaran, C., Chisnall, B., Drakatos, P., Sivakumar, S., Sivakumar, B., Barrecheguren, M., ... & Steier, J. (2014). A cross-sectional survey investigating the desensitisation of graphic health warning labels and their impact on smokers, non-smokers and patients with COPD in a London cohort. BMJ open, 4(7), e004782.

**Step 2**  Date: ...... / ...... / ......

# My Brain's Journey Toward Change

**In order to change my eating behaviors, how should my brain change over time?**

Before starting any program, we must first know what steps lie ahead. How long will it take to reach our goal? What activities should we undertake along the route?

It's important to know that success in weight-loss treatment programs requires time and energy. Maybe you've made efforts to lose weight in the past, but you failed each time. Two possible reasons for failure may be not knowing what to expect along the journey, and what steps you need to take in order to achieve your goal. Perhaps you even asked yourself when you began to read this book, is this the same method other treatments use? Will I fail again? How long does it take to reach the ideal weight? If I lose weight, I probably won't be able to keep it off! Questions and worries such as these may make it difficult for you to start your journey.

In this session, we want to discuss the issue of overweight in a different way, but first, please answer the following questions:

✎ **What do you think are features of a healthy weight loss program? Common expectations for weight loss might be:**

1. I want to see the results, very fast and I want to lighten myself for my brother's wedding which is in two months' time.  Yes ☐  No ☐
2. I don't want a strict program. I'm tired of long diets. Every time I start a diet, I get angry.  Yes ☐  No ☐
3. Permanent change, I'm tired of regaining weight after ending or giving up on the diet. I hope to find a way to maintain weight. Loss, and not regain the weight.  Yes ☐  No ☐
4. Adjusting my lifestyle, so that I do not need a diet. My dream is to find a way to lose weight without a diet.  Yes ☐  No ☐
5. 
6. 

In this book, we will try to provide you with the proper conditions for a successful long-term change. Now think about the next question.

✎ **What are the differences between you and people who are at an ideal weight? Here are some common answers. Mark answers you agree with ☑**

1. They are lucky and do not gain weight no matter what they eat. I have friends who eat three times as much as I do and don't get fat. ☐
2. They do not enjoy eating. Skinny people are often forced to eat and they do not enjoy eating like the rest of us. ☐
3. They get more exercise, but I do not have the time or energy for exercise. ☐
4. They are genetically lean, but I gain weight if I even look at food! ☐
5. 
6. 

## Golden features of the healthy weight loss program in this book

1. It's based on **awareness** and **brain empowerment**.

2. People are not supposed to have a lifespan diet. **Deprivation of the pleasure of eating is not the purpose of this program.**

3. The program is not tiresom and you will **enjoy** the process.

4. Persond values are prioritized and you will find **your own path**.

5. Ultimately, **profound**, **gradual** and **stable** changes will happen in your eating behavior.

In order to figure out the correct answers to the above questions, you need to change your attitude toward being overweight. The first question to consider is, "Why did I become obese? And why, despite using different methods, do I regain any weight that I lose?" In response, one might think: "Maybe your brain is more dependent on eating than other people's." Overweight people are usually preoccupied with eating. Delicious foods strongly attract them. In many cases, if they are away from home for a few hours, they begin thinking about their next meal and worry about getting hungry. Being overweight or obese may be the result of your brain's dependence on eating. In other words, what you really need to do isn't to change your weight alone, but to manage your brain's dependency on food.

One of the important differences between obese and lean people, is this dependency on food and eating. Lean people are not generally concerned about eating and don't tend to eat large quantities of food, but this does not mean they're not getting hungry or don't need to eat. Rather, it means that they're not dependent on eating, and when confronted with food, they're not as preoccupied with it as the majority of obese people are.

**Features of dependency are listed in the table below.**

### General Features of Being Dependent to Something (i.e., food or etc.)

**1 Gaining pleasure:** When you enjoy doing something, you're likely to be more dependent on it over time.

**2 Compulsion:** Sometimes your dependency changes in a way that does not make you feel pleasure, but failing to do it will make you feel bad and unpleasant. So, you feel compelled to do that.

**3 Expecting pleasure while exposing triggers:** Although dependent individuals may enjoy eating less than others, they are more vulnerable when exposed to triggers.

**4 Ignoring the side effects:** Dependency can make an individual's interpretation of events so distorted that they disregard or fail to see harmful effects.

**5 Activating under stress conditions:** If you are dependent on a behavior, you are more likely to take refuge in that behavior during stressful situations to calm yourself.

As you already know, the urge to eat, food craving, and uncontrolled overeating are all results of what's happening inside your brain. Therefore, a successful weight loss program should include changes in the function of the brain (a.k.a. cognitive processes), because when your brain processes, the information about eating in a different way, your attitudes toward food and behavior will change as well.

If your brain continues to process your relationship to food and eating as it always has, losing weight will be a painful matter, and restricting your diet will be difficult, if not impossible. You may have restricted your intake many times and failed; that's because you embarked on your diet plan without preparation, and suddenly decided to eliminate lots of food-related behaviors. How can a person who has eaten whatever pleasurable suddenly prevent themselves from eating anything? It's an unrealistic expectation, and if you have not been able to stay the course, it's not due to weak willpower. Major changes, without preparation, are almost impossible for any person to maintain because that's not how our brains are wired.

We do not intend to give you a diet with lots of limitations; rather, we aim to give you self-awareness regarding your thinking, attitudes, behaviors, and eating habits, as well as identifying the factors, conditions, and even relationships that lead to overeating. On this journey, we will instruct you on how your brain and its cognitive processes work in relation to food. Scientists call this oversight of your own cognitive processes, "metacognition". The greater your metacognition of eating behaviors becomes, the better you will be able to change your relationship with food.

Naturally, starting any program of change will seem hard at first. You may be confused about where to start or think you should change everything at once. However, in this book, you will learn the essential skills for changing your thoughts and behaviors. You will familiarize yourself with your brain's resistance to change during the treatment program, and you will learn the skills for getting through that resistance. In other words, we want your brain to command you to eat enough, and when your body really needs food.

### Eating management skills

In fact, eating "only so much" and "only when necessary" is a skill that requires much learning and practice. It's natural for you not to have the skill to manage your eating behavior at the start of the program. Learning this skill – along with other skills such as learning to drive or play a musical instrument – requires training and practice. If you want to be a skillful driver, simply knowing the basics of how to drive a car and being familiar with the rules is not enough – you have to practice for hours. The more time you spend on it, the more skillful you will become. However, it's important to note that you can't drive for hours on a single day and expect your skills to be greatly improved the following day. If you divide this training time over several days, though, your skills will increase over the next few days. So, to learn any skill, a certain length of time is also required. You can't expect yourself to master eating management skills by just resisting eating for a day or even several.

In fact, by using the "cold turkey" method, the brain and body are faced with deprivation, which can actually cause cravings to get stronger. Not only will you regain any weight loss, but your cravings may also be stronger than before, and in the end, after several periods of deprivation, your weight may even multiply. Unfortunately, this is a method often used in weight loss regimes, and many people have already been hurt by it. So, if you are ever concerned about the length of this treatment journey, remember that strengthening eating management skills and becoming a new person takes time and that days, weeks, and months may be needed for you to learn these skills through practice. You have to wait patiently, like a gardener who plants a sapling and regularly attends to it. You may not be able to observe its daily growth, but you know that this sapling will be a tree one day, and will be admired by everyone.

The period of "Brain Obesity" workbook you're reading is a minimum of six months. In the first months, you will become more familiar with your thoughts and behaviors while eating, and you'll learn how to change your behaviors and habits gradually. Meanwhile, you will be losing weight while changing your eating habits over time.

**Brain Box**

# What's going on in your brain?

Before reading this section, think about the following questions:

- Am I aware of everything that happens in my brain?
- How does the dependent brain in humans take control of the individual, without being aware of it?

Look closely at the image below for 5 seconds. What is the difference between these two images?

If we ask you, which of these images is more attractive? What answer will you give?

In a study, these two questions were asked of the participants. In response to the first question, most people answered that there is no difference. The truth is that the pupil size is different in these two images, and the left image has a larger pupil. But in a short time, the human brain is incapable of explicitly finding this difference in most cases. In response to the second question, when these images were displayed individually, most people gave a higher score to the left image (the image with the larger pupil) as a more attractive image. In fact, when assessing the amount of attractiveness, the human brain system has different feelings toward these two images but when consciously discerning the difference, it is unable to find an answer. Why is this happening? In order to investigate this, they put people in the brain scanner and asked the questions at the same time as the pictures were displayed for a few seconds and noticed the activity of the region of the brain that distinguishes between these images while one does not notice this distinction. This region is called amygdala. In fact, the amygdala is more active in large pupil condition. This means the amygdala recognizes this difference, but this information is not available at a conscious level. So, there are regions in the brain that do not function at our level of consciousness, a phenomenon that eating behaviors are strongly associated with. For example, there are times when we are not supposed to eat anything, but may eat anyway without knowing why. We know that we are overweight which causes harm to our body, but we unconsciously crave food. The basic question is: Are there any strategies to manage these regions that are beyond our consciousness? The answer is **yes**, you will learn through this book to move your feelings and desires into your conscious realm.

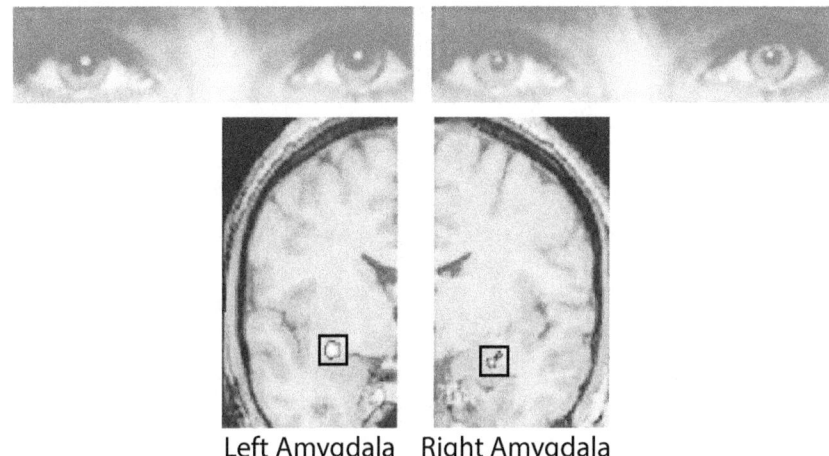

Left Amygdala   Right Amygdala

Date: ...... / ...... / ......

# Your Own Footsteps on this Journey

**1** To become familiar with the differences in the brain's response to food and the cognitive processes of a food-dependent person before and after completing this journey for change, complete the following table.

| Features of a food-dependent person | Thoughts of a food-dependent person before change | Thoughts of that person after a change |
|---|---|---|
| Craving sweets when seeing a large pastry | Wow, I wish I had a pastry! I wish I could eat sweets and not get fat. | These sweets can be harmful to my health. It's better to leave this place, so sweets won't provoke my brain unnecessarily. |
| Feeling sad after a short period of reducing consumption of fatty and sugary food. | Without delicious foods, sorrow will overwhelm me! If losing weight is going to make my life so depressing, I'd rather stay fat. | I used to think that eating was the only way to enjoy life. How dangerous that was for my health! I need to try to find new ways to enjoy life. |
| Hating his/her obese body and eating even more, or carrying out other unhealthy behaviors to reduce that negative feeling. | I don't like my fat body. I actually hate it, but I have no other option. Eating helps me forget this pain. | I love my body. I'm a happy chubby. I know that with my acceptance and commitment to change, my body will change along with my brain. |

**2** In addition to the examples below, what do you think you can change about yourself or your environment to facilitate your brain's journey to change? How much time do you think will be needed for these changes?

| Important changes in yourself | Time needed |
|---|---|
| Eating won't be the most important and only fun aspect of my life. | 6 months |
| I will walk every evening at 6 p.m. on my way home. | 1 month |
| The first step of change is self-awareness. So, I will try to visit a professional therapist. | A year |

| Important changes in your environment | Time needed |
|---|---|
| The fridge won't be full of fatty junk foods. | 3 months |
| I will write down my shopping list, before entering the supermarket so I do not make unnecessary purchases. | 2 months |
| Large dishes will be replaced by small dishes. | 1 week |

**3** Individuals experience varying degrees of craving. Awareness of these individual differences plays an important role in your level of craving. This self-awareness is the success key to the treatment. As you begin your health journey by reading this book, try to find out more about yourself by answering these questions:

A) Questionnaire to assess the characteristics and severity of your cravings in general: Please read each of the following sentences carefully and then select a number from 1 to 6 (in accordance with the guide below), specifying the extent to which the sentence is generally applicable to you.

For example: Being with someone who is eating makes me hungry.

| Never | Rarely | Sometimes | Regularly | Often | Always |
|---|---|---|---|---|---|
| ① | ② | ③ | ④ | ⑤ | ⑥ |

1. When I crave something to eat, I know I won't be able to stop eating once I start.
2. If I eat something that I'm craving, I often lose control and eat too much.
3. I hate surrendering to my cravings.
4. Food cravings invariably make me think of ways to get what I want to eat.
5. I feel like I have food on my mind all the time.

**6.** I experience guilt because of the cravings I have for food.

**7.** I find myself preoccupied with food.

**8.** I eat to feel better.

**9.** Eating makes everything seem much better.

**10.** Thinking about my favorite food makes my mouth water.

**11.** Even when I'm not hungry, I crave food.

**12.** I feel as if my body wants me to eat tasty food.

**13.** I get so hungry that nothing seems to satiate me.

**14.** Eating what I crave makes me feel better.

**15.** When I satisfy my cravings, I feel less depressed.

**16.** Eating what I crave makes me feel guilty.

**17.** Whenever I have cravings, I find myself making plans to eat.

**18.** Eating makes me calm.

**19.** I crave foods when I feel bored, angry, or sad.

**20.** I feel less anxious after I eat.

**21.** If I get what I'm craving, I can't stop myself from eating it.

**22.** When I crave some special food, I usually try to eat it as soon as possible.

**23.** When I eat what I crave, I feel great.

**24.** I have no will power to resist my food cravings.

**25.** Once I start eating, I have trouble stopping.

**26.** I can't stop thinking about eating no matter how hard I try.

**27.** I spend way too much time thinking about what I should eat next.

**Total score:** _____

## B) Questionnaire for assessing the severity of your craving at this moment:

**1.** At the moment, I have an intense desire to eat something tasty.

**2.** At the moment, I'm craving tasty food.

**3.** At the moment, I'm under pressure to eat one or more specific foods.

**4.** At the moment, eating something tasty would make things just perfect.

**5.** At the moment, if I were to eat what I desire, I'm sure my mood would improve.

**6.** At the moment, eating something tasty would feel wonderful.

**7.** At the moment, if I ate something, I wouldn't feel so sluggish and lethargic.

**8.** At the moment, satisfying my appetite would make me feel less grouchy and irritable.

**9.** At the moment, I would feel more alert if I could satisfy my appetite.

**10.** At the moment, if I had something tasty to eat, I wouldn't be able to stop eating it.

**11.** At the moment, my desire to eat something tasty seems overpowering.

**12.** At the moment, I know I'm going to keep on thinking about tasty food until I actually have some.

**13.** At the moment, if I ate right now, my stomach wouldn't feel so empty.

**14.** At the moment, I feel weak because I haven't eaten in a while.

**15.** At the moment, I feel hungry.

**Total score:** ...............

After completing these two questionnaires, if you feel that you're having problems with your cravings, follow along in the book. We will teach you tools to manage those cravings.

If you've gone on a diet several times and failed, don't be afraid of trying a new way. Tell yourself that if you have not been able to reach your goal, it wasn't your fault; instead, it was your route that sabotaged you. Now that you're on the right route, start again from the beginning, but believe in it this time. On this route, along with weight changes, there will also be self-changes, in order to ensure that you reach your goal and maintain your desired weight.

| Day | Monday | Tuesday | Wednesday | Thursday | Friday | Saturday | Sunday |
|---|---|---|---|---|---|---|---|
| Weight | / / | / / | / / | / / | / / | / / | / / |

**Daily Weight Table**

## Summary

1. Changing eating behavior is a long and complex journey requiring time, energy, and commitment. Its final result is very valuable.
2. Eating behavior management is a skill that emerges from increasing awareness and practice over time.
3. Enjoying your brain's journey toward change is an important factor in achieving success.
4. The difference between you and people who are not overweight is your brain's dependency on eating.
5. By enhancing the brain, and identifying and modifying the brain's dependency on eating, you will reform your eating behavior over time.
6.
7.

8.

---

If you want to read more

1. Amemiya, S., & Ohtomo, K. (2012). Effect of the observed pupil size on the amygdala of the beholders. Social cognitive and affective neuroscience, 7(3), 332–341. https://doi.org/10.1093/scan/nsr013

2. Demos, K. E., Kelley, W. M., Ryan, S. L., Davis, F. C., & Whalen, P. J. (2008). Human amygdala sensitivity to the pupil size of others. Cerebral cortex (New York, N.Y. : 1991), 18(12), 2729–2734. https://doi.org/10.1093/cercor/bhn034

3. da Costa Carvalho, S. Q., de Andrade, M. J. O., & dos Santos, N. A. (2019). Relationship between facial attractiveness and pupil diameter in young adults. Psico, 50(2), 30033.

> **Step 3**  Date: ... / ... / ...

# Food Craving vs. Hunger

**Is the feeling of desiring or craving food the same as hunger?**

In this session, you will become familiar with the concepts of "hunger" and "cravings" and the differences between them. It's normal for you to eat a variety of different foods at different times and under different conditions, but you're not necessarily hungry every time you eat. Hunger occurs when you have not eaten for a few hours and your stomach is empty, your blood sugar has dropped, and your body sends "need messages" to the brain. In this case, you may be willing to eat any kind of food in order to respond to your hunger. People sometimes say they would even be willing to eat a dried out crust of bread.

You may have experienced this situation many times: you go home for lunch, but you don't have anything on hand, and you're very hungry. In this situation, you might snack on a few pieces of bread to tide you over while preparing your lunch. Other times, you eat not because of hunger or because you want to satisfy your real needs, but rather because there is a desire or craving for food. Sometimes this is simply in response to the presence of a certain food. When you see food, or smell it, or think about it, you will tend to eat it. In this case, it's said that you desire that food, but when the desire grows, it is called craving.

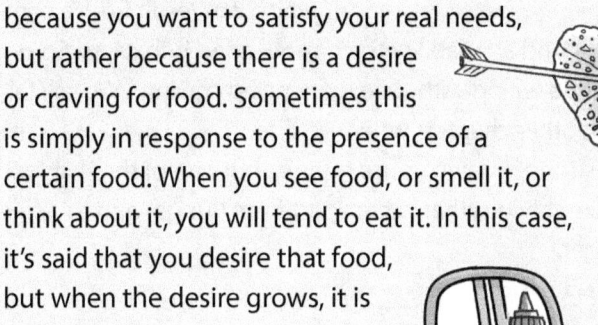

During a state of craving, your brain is preoccupied with eating a particular food. If you don't eat it, the idea of eating won't just go away. This is the difference between a desire and a craving. This condition is frequently seen in people with food dependency. Sometimes you may be able to resist this temptation, but often you will succumb to it, especially when your cravings are very strong. In this case, resistance to craving is very difficult and many people cannot withstand it. Sometimes not responding to craving creates an unpleasant feeling, but as soon as the craving is satisfied, this unpleasant feeling goes away and may even be replaced with a sense of comfort and pleasure. Eating in response to cravings is not always about enjoying the food, but on many occasions, we respond to cravings in order to avoid the negative feelings associated with not responding to them! Sometimes people will even end up experiencing the extremely unpleasant sensation of being too full after responding to a craving, but they still give in to it the next time. Sometimes your craving isn't slowed down by eating – it seems that, no matter what you eat, it's not enough, and this causes overeating which can lead to feelings of discomfort.

Perhaps you've experienced this feeling many times, or heard from others: "I don't get satisfied, no matter what I eat", and "I eat so much that I get tired or get a stomachache. Then it's time to stop eating, but my eyes are still looking for food." This is called "unrestricted overeating" or "binge eating", which can result from a combination of intense cravings and an inability to control eating behaviors. Sometimes people engage in binge eating without experiencing cravings. We will talk about this phenomenon in other chapters when we discuss "habitual eating". It's normal for cravings to be stronger when you're hungry, but one of the skills you need to learn is to recognize cravings that occur apart from hunger and to differentiate that from real hunger.

In order to learn this skill, please do the exercises in the following step carefully.

### Please name a few situations where you experience real hunger, such as the examples below:

| | | |
|---|---|---|
| 1. Days when I leave home without having breakfast. | Yes ☐ | No ☐ |
| 2. At noon, after doing housework. | Yes ☐ | No ☐ |
| 3. After two hours of exercise. | Yes ☐ | No ☐ |
| 4. After a four-hour hike. | Yes ☐ | No ☐ |
| 5. | | |
| 6. | | |

✎ **Please name a few situations where you experience craving without hunger, such as the examples below:**

1 At a wedding, when I see cream puffs on the table.      Yes ☐      No ☐
2 When I open the refrigerator and see sausage or deli meat. Yes ☐   No ☐
3 When I smell freshly-baked bread at the house.         Yes ☐      No ☐
4 When my mom cooks and the whole room abounds the aroma of food.
                                                          Yes ☐      No ☐
5
6

Hunger and feelings of satiety are completely normal, and normal-weight people with no eating problems as well as those who are overweight will experience both. Craving is also normal and is seen in almost all people, but it is usually more powerful and disabling in obese people, and they find it difficult to resist. Most people experience desires and cravings – the problem lies in surrendering to them. People with eating problems experience a great deal of craving and usually cannot cope with it, and this results in weight gain.

✎ **Please think carefully about how you feel and how you behave when you are hungry and when you are experiencing various levels of craving (intense to weak). Write an experience for each one.**

If you want to, then score from 0 to 100 points the unpleasant feelings resulting from any of these items. What score do you give each? The following table is a sample of answers given by people to these questions.

| Condition | Describe your feelings, thoughts, and behaviors | Unpleasantness score |
|---|---|---|
| **Hunger** | my stomach burns and I feel nauseous | 70 |
| **Weak craving** | I have cravings, but I can stop myself | 40 |
| **Intense craving** | I can't bring myself to do anything and I don't feel calm until I eat my desired food | 90 |

It is interesting that people have very different experiences of hunger and craving. Some experience hunger infrequently, while others might experience it once or twice during the day.

The experience of craving is very different in different people as well. Some people never have intense cravings while some other people regularly find themselves eating special foods such as cookies or macaroni and cheese because of a disabling craving. Which of these groups are you in?

I rarely experience cravings ○

I find myself craving foods once or twice a day ○

I feel cravings almost all the time ○

✎ **The table below shows some differences between cravings and hunger. Please think about some of your own items:**

| Hunger | Cravings |
|---|---|
| I feel hungry when I haven't eaten in at least three hours | I crave certain foods more |
| When hungry, my stomach rumbles/growls | Even if I'm not hungry, I'll still eat my favorite food |
| It doesn't matter to me what I eat when I'm hungry | When I see delicious food, even if I'm full, I can eat some of it |
| When I'm hungry and I eat, I feel satisfied | When I overeat due to my cravings, I feel guilty |
| When hungry, I feel like my stomach is empty | Although I've responded to my craving and eaten my favorite food, I'd still like to eat more |
| When hungry, I feel weak and cannot do anything | When I see delicious food, my brain becomes preoccupied with it |
| After a few hours of hunger, the feeling goes away | When I crave a particular food, I lose my head till I eat it |
| When I'm hungry, I do not look forward to socializing | When I'm with my friends and family, cravings start |
| When I'm full, seeing people eating does not encourage me to eat | Watching people enjoy eating makes me crave food |

One of the main lessons of this book is to learn to distinguish hunger from cravings and to learn to respond normally to hunger while preventing or inhibiting cravings. Failure to respond to hunger will ultimately make your brain and body greedier and, over time, you will fail to lose weight or regain any weight you've lost. One of the main strategies for managing frequent hunger is to set up an eating schedule throughout the day. If you eat breakfast, lunch, and dinner every day at a regular hour, you won't feel hunger irregularly. As a result, it will be easier to identify cravings and to restrain them.

### Brain Box
# What's going on in your brain?

Before reading this section, think about the following questions:

- Do you crave for a special food and feel nervous till you eat it?
- Why some people in stimulating situations like a barbeque party only eat a few bites and say it's enough for them, but others eat themselves to death?

In this section, you will get acquainted with two essential body systems: The need system and the pleasure system; the other name of the need system is homeostasis; it means uniformity and stability, which refers to the desire of an organism to maintain its internal stability. For example, the concentration of calcium, protein, or sugar in the blood. On the other hand, there is a hedonic system (pleasure) for every living creature that guarantees its survival over time, such as reproduction.

The basic principle of balance between these two systems is that pleasure must be dominated by homeostasis so the organism can survive over time. But the pleasure system sometimes works against or resists homeostasis, and its activities may not benefit other systems of the body. But why does this happen?

If we take a look at the evolution of human beings, perhaps in some stages, they had to do

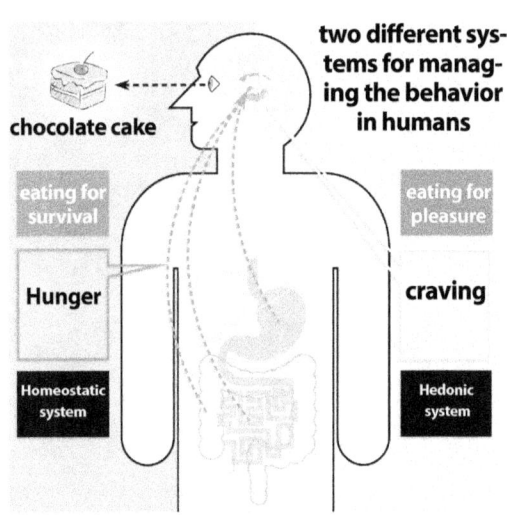

things for the survival of the next generation, even if it did not favor the need system of the individual, or led to their death.

In this model, we're not going to make people eat anything; on the contrary, eating should happen, but enough, and according to the body's needs. In fact, we manage and inhibit the system of pleasure and do not respond to craving, but we need to respond properly to hunger and the need system.

Many overweight people lose the ability to recognize the signals of these two systems within their bodies over time, but we will regain this ability during this course.

Date: ...... / ...... / ......

## Your Own Footsteps on this Journey...

**1** In the table below, please make a note of what you experienced and how you behaved when exposed to the trigger (whatever initiates or ignites your craving) and the way the craving feels.

| Time | Place | Trigger | Experience |
|---|---|---|---|
| 9 A.M. | At work | Seeing breakfast foods | Although I'd eaten breakfast, seeing the breakfast buffet at work made me crave it, so I ate a few bites even though I wasn't hungry |
| 4 P.M. | Cafe | Seeing my friend eating a chocolate cake | Seeing her appetite made me crave for some hot chocolate |
| 10 P.M | At home | Watching some advertisement about new flavored chips | The sound of crunching potato chips makes me want to try some, but it was hard to buy it at that moment, so I prepare some home-made popcorn. |

**2** **During the time between reading this step and the next step, please write down some of your experiences of craving and hunger.**

*a) On Thursday, I had to wake up early, but my alarm didn't sound. So after getting up, I was in a hurry and I didn't have time to eat breakfast. About 11 A.M. I felt terribly hungry.*

*b) On Sunday, I had been invited to a barbeque party. Although I had eaten enough at home, seeing those baby-back ribs, I couldn't help but eat some.*

**3** **What are some strategies you can use in your own life to distinguish hunger from craving and respond to both of them properly?**

*Example: a) Body scanning while seeing my favorite food, briefly after having lunch, and compare it with the moment I haven't eaten for a long time.*
*b) Trying to have small healthy snacks, in order not to feel hungry between meals.*
*c) Trying to keep my mind busy with things I love, (like painting or listening to music) while experiencing cravings.*

A complete avoidance of desired foods is one of the most common reasons for diet failure.

During the first few steps of the book, you may feel more food cravings than usual. This phenomenon is perfectly normal and indicates your brain is actively considering the content of this book. You will see over time that by increasing your awareness and commitment to change, your feelings of craving will be changed. Stay with us.

| Day | Monday | Tuesday | Wednesday | Thursday | Friday | Saturday | Sunday |
|---|---|---|---|---|---|---|---|
| Weight | / / | / / | / / | / / | / / | / / | / / |

**Daily Weight Table**

## Summary

1. There is a difference in the experience of hunger and craving that you may not be able to distinguish.
2. In this therapeutic course, our goal is not to endanger you with long-lasting hunger and food deprivation.
3. Long-term starvation will make you vulnerable to craving and it will disturb your weight loss process.
4. Our goal is to learn how to distinguish between cravings and hunger, then to learn to manage those cravings while responding to hunger.
5. 
6. 

---

If you want to read more

1. Lutter, M., & Nestler, E. J. (2009). Homeostatic and hedonic signals interact in the regulation of food intake. The Journal of nutrition, 139(3), 629-632.

2. Saper, C. B., Chou, T. C., & Elmquist, J. K. (2002). The need to feed: homeostatic and hedonic control of eating. Neuron, 36(2), 199-211.

3. Stroebe, W., Papies, E. K., & Aarts, H. (2008). From homeostatic to hedonic theories of eating: Self-regulatory failure in food-rich environments. Applied Psychology, 57, 172-193.

4. Luca, F., Perry, G. H., & Di Rienzo, A. (2010). Evolutionary adaptations to dietary changes. Annual review of nutrition, 30, 291–314. https://doi.org/10.1146/annurev-nutr-080508-141048

5. Zucoloto, F. S. (2011). Evolution of the human feeding behavior. Psychology & Neuroscience, 4(1), 131-141.

| Step 4 | Date:  /  / |

# Triggers and Craving Response

**How does overeating begin?**

Have you ever felt that even though you're not hungry, you want to eat again? As we discussed in the previous step, not every eating behavior corresponds to a genuine need for nutrients. This may happen to you. Even though you're not hungry, you see delicious food or sweets and you indulge in the opportunity! Or when you go to the grocery store and see different foods, you feel the urge to eat them, so even though they're not on your shopping list, you'll buy some. As you can see, in many cases, eating begins even when there is no need for it. We will refer to any environmental, social, or psychological stimulants and the feelings that cause us to eat as "triggers". Eating triggers usually play an important role in excessive calorie intake and subsequently, being overweight. All of these symptoms, conditions, and situations are triggers that cause unnecessary eating.

✎ **Here is a list of eating triggers. Please read them carefully and check the ones which apply to you:**

1. The smell of food, especially your favorite foods ☐
2. Seeing a variety of sweets in the bakery ☐
3. Seeing a variety of foods on the dining table ☐
4. Seeing people eat ☐
5. Hearing your friend describe a delicious meal ☐
6. Eating with a group of people ☐
7. Seeing or eating potato chips with dip ☐
8. Feeling tense or anxious ☐
9. Going to the supermarket and seeing the prepared food ☐
10. Staying home alone ☐
11. Being sad ☐
12. Thinking about a delicious meal you've eaten ☐
13. Being joyful ☐
14. Reading a detailed menu of a good restaurant ☐
15. Feeling tired ☐
16. Remembering a dinner party with stimulating foods ☐
17. Being unable to sleep (having insomnia) ☐
18. Having a mental preoccupation ☐
19. Seeing a box of chocolates on the table ☐
20. Being angry and upset ☐
21. Just before and/or during your menstrual cycle (women) ☐

Now, a question: **How do eating triggers work? Why are you drawn into eating when dealing with triggers?** At first sight, the relationship seems to be stimulus (trigger)-and-response (eating behavior), and it can be concluded that whatever is eatable will make us eat. But this relationship isn't that simple in our brains. After exposure to a trigger, a thought is formed in your brain, which then causes a desire to eat, and then this desire, or craving, is converted into motivation for eating. In other words, that relationship is as follows: trigger ▶ thought ▶ craving ▶ eating behavior. Therefore, one of the steps we must take at the beginning of our weight loss journey is to identify the triggers for eating and, thus, the thoughts that result from them.

**For example, as soon as you see a box of chocolates, you eat some of them. What seems to be happening is this:**

**But in fact, what really happened is this:**

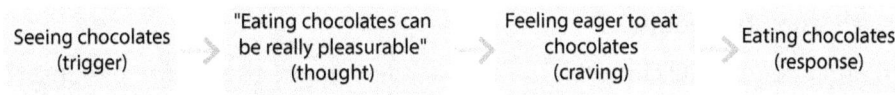

This process happens so quickly that sometimes you don't even notice. You've gone on a diet many times, but despite the fact that you want to avoid overeating, suddenly you find yourself in the middle of binge eating and you have no idea of what's going on and why you eat so much. We feel that it's important for you to keep in mind the mental process shown in the above diagram throughout your weight loss treatment.

Careful attention to this chart shows that certain foods are not delicious by themselves but our thoughts, beliefs, and interpretation determine the level of craving for food. For example, each of you may have different feelings about pizza, pasta, steak, or any other food according to the memories and experiences you have in life. If pizza or steak has been an integral part of your family and your childhood memories, it is natural to have a positive opinion of them which will cause you to crave. Imagine someone who lives abroad and has never experienced a Sunday barbecue. This person may not have any propensity to eat these types of food. You may have never liked a certain food in the past, but after getting married or moving to a new country, and eating that food with your spouse or friends you begin to create positive memories. Over time, eating that particular food will become a particular pleasure, and you will desire to relive those experiences.

This is why cravings are different from person to person or can change over time for an individual. Therefore, if you want to avoid eating regretful foods, you must change your interpretations of that food. In this step, the goal is to become aware of your mental interpretations. In the next steps, we will discuss how to modify them.

**For more information about this process, look at the following examples:**

The smell of barbeque (trigger) when you pass a restaurant might produce these series of thoughts: "What a wonderful smell of roasting meat!" "It's been a while since I've eaten any barbeque." "It smells as if high-quality meat was used to make this restaurant's barbecue." "The air is filled with the smell of roasting meat – it would melt in my mouth!" "Last month, I went to a restaurant and ate some delicious barbeque." "Eating this restaurant's barbeque would make me feel good."

Seeing ice-cream in the freezer: This is the last time carton of ice cream I will eat, I won't buy another?

Being offered a delicious cheesecake: If I reject them, they might get upset?

Sitting at a big dinner party table: One night doesn't affect the rest of my life?

It's likely that answering these questions may be challenging for you, because – as has been said – the process that occurs in the mind is so fast that you may not have noticed your thoughts while eating, or you didn't even know that there might be specific thoughts about this issue in your brain. Acquiring the skill of recognizing each of the four steps in the above diagram is one of the important "self-awareness skills" that you need in order to overcome overeating. You should be able to recall your overeating behaviors over the past few days and select those which were due to triggers. Next, carefully review all the events as if they were a movie in slow motion, so you can observe the procedure step by step: from the trigger to thought, thought to craving, and craving to eating. Over time, as you gradually study the other steps in this book, you will be able to identify triggers throughout the day, be aware of the thoughts arising from those triggers, feel the formation and power of your craving, and record the final result of this food-trigger exposure, (which, in cases of failure, might be eating). This conscious look at overeating caused by triggers is one of the most important skills needed to manage the overeating.

Brain Box
# What's going on in your brain?
Before reading this section, think about the following questions:

- Why is it that when we see our favorite food, we start eating without realizing what's going on?
- How do people react to food in different situations? (sometimes controling but in many cases, overeating!)

As explained in this section, there are some triggers in your surroundings that may be unique to you, such as ice cream, cheesecake, and pizza. Sometimes you are exposed to them and find yourself in the middle of eating them. What's happening in your brain?

When your brain perceives an eating trigger, some areas in the deep parts of the brain are activated; areas known as the limbic system (lower brain). This system is the basis of our emotional life, emotional behaviors, and motivations. In addition, many of these areas play an important role in the process of memory and data storage and some have close links with the olfactory system, which may explain why some things are particularly enjoyable. The most important area of the limbic system as we mentioned earlier is the amygdala. The limbic system is often controlled by the areas in the upper regions of the brain's prefrontal cortex, however, it can operate independently, which is referred to as "bottom up regulation". In bottom- up regulation, the amygdala and other deep areas of the brain give an intense and quick response to the trigger and facilitate the perceptual process by guiding attention to it. This process is leferred to as the outbursting. In many cases, the prefrontal areas (higher regions) control the outbreak, but sometimes the regulation from "top to bottom" will fail and the eating will occur. As noted in the previous steps, activity in the limbic area occurs outside of our conscious experience.

Let's make it clearer with a simple example: When

**the prefrontal circuits involved in inhibiting craving**

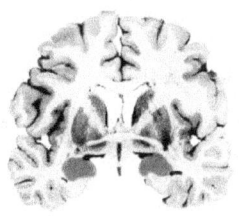 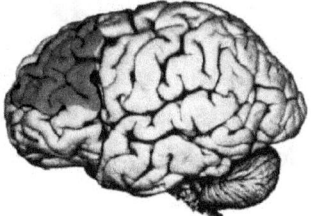

Bottom-up Craving   Top-down Control

you are exposed to a variety of foods, all foods are perceived by your brain, but in the meantime, one of the foods may be processed differently according to your previous experiences. For example, the emotional connection you have with the pizza and its memories may not be the same with chicken fries, and this unconscious process occurs in the limbic system and creates such an outbreak in your brain without waiting till the other brain regions analyze the situation; this process turns all of your attention to the food and sends its decision to movement areas of the brain, so your brain is locked and it does not react to anything else unless it is related to that food. In this situation, you do not know why, but you find yourself in the middle of eating your favorite meal at a party and if we ask you why, you would probably justify your eating habits as: I have made up my mind to please myself just for a moment, or, after a wakeup call, I find myself preoccupied with food.

Date: ...... / ...... / ......

## Your Own Footsteps on this Journey...

**1** **Write down a complete list of triggers you encountered since you completed Step 3.**

1. Example: Felt depressed and upset after a quarrel with a close friend on Monday.
2. Felt helpless and tired after having a hard day at work.
3. Facing pressure at work on Tuesday.
4. ................................................................................................
5. ................................................................................................
6. ................................................................................................
7. ................................................................................................
8. ................................................................................................
9. ................................................................................................
10. ...............................................................................................

**2** **What are your personal triggers that induce more "hot thoughts,"(in which a person's thinking is influenced by their emotional state) which ultimately causes a food craving?**

1. Seeing chocolate ice-cream
2. Checking food related posts in social media
3. Being ignored from my friends
4. ................................................

| 5  | 13 |
|----|----|
| 6  | 14 |
| 7  | 15 |
| 8  | 16 |
| 9  | 17 |
| 10 | 18 |
| 11 | 19 |
| 12 | 20 |

**3** **Pay attention to your eating behaviors during this week, and make notes below regarding your thoughts, feelings, and behavior when you are faced with eating triggers:**

| trigger | thought | feeling | behavior |
|---|---|---|---|
| Seeing a food post on Instagram | How delicious melted cheese would taste right now | Pleasure, Guilt | Leaving the app. Drinking a glass of water, Eating an apple |
| Seeing preparation of a kebab while crossing the street | It would be a taste of heaven | Joy | Keep on walking and window shopping |

Studies have shown that people who do not eat breakfast are four and a half times more likely to become obese? Why? Can you guess at the cause?

For overweight people, weighing in can be associated with many negative feelings such as stress, sadness, and guilt. Therefore, people consciously or unconsciously avoid weighing. You need to remember that the first step in solving a problem is accepting the existence of the problem without making a negative judgment about it.

| Day | Monday | Tuesday | Wednesday | Thursday | Friday | Saturday | Sunday |
|---|---|---|---|---|---|---|---|
| | / / | / / | / / | / / | / / | / / | / / |
| Weight | | | | | | | |

Daily Weight Table

## Summary

1. Triggers do not mean anything by themselves. Our memories, experiences, traditions, and beliefs influence the meanings we give to these triggers.

2. The meaning you give to the triggers in your environment will cause you to crave a particular food, but it is not the same for every person.

3. If you want to have a new experience when confronted with delicious food, you should first understand the beliefs, interpretations, and judgments of your own about those foods and plan to change or modify them.

4. When your brain perceives an eating trigger, some areas with emotional basis in the deep parts of the brain are activated; areas known as the limbic system (bottom up regulation). This system is often controlled by the upper regions of the brain (top to bottom). If the regulation from top to bottom fails, the eating will occur.

5. 

---

If you want to read more

1. Sanders, N., Smeets, P. A., van Elburg, A. A., Danner, U. N., van Meer, F., Hoek, H. W., & Adan, R. A. (2015). Altered food-cue processing in chronically ill and recovered women with anorexia nervosa. Frontiers in Behavioral Neuroscience, 9, 46.

2. Urdapilleta, I., Mirabel-Sarron, C., Meunier, J. M., & Richard, J. F. (2005). Study of the categorization process among patients with eating disorders: A new cognitive approach to psychopathology. L'Encephale, 31(1 Pt 1), 82-91.

### Step 5  Date: ..... / ..... / .....

# Food Cues in Our Environment that Make Us Eat More and More

**How does our environment make us eat?**

If you remember, in the third session, you became familiar with the definition of eating triggers. In this session, we intend to examine these triggers in more detail. Generally, triggers are divided into two categories: "Food Cues," which will be discussed in this section, and "Emotional Triggers," which will be discussed in later sessions. Food cues are further divided into three categories: environmental, social, and imagery.

1. Environmental food cues: Examples of environmental cues are pictures, scenes, smells, and tastes that make you crave food, such as seeing or smelling your favorite food, seeing a food advertisement, watching a cooking program, seeing snacks in a supermarket, or tasting a sample of pickles or sweets.

**2. Social food cues:** There have been many times that you were reluctant to eat, but because you saw others eating, your appetite was stimulated. Or, despite being full while sitting next to a person who is eating, you'll try a few bites. Or at a gathering or party, you meet friends who are eating, you overeat unconsciously. All of these situations involve social cues, meaning social conditions, relationships, or people who make you crave food.

**3. Imagery food cues:** Recalling pleasant memories of eating favorite foods or picturing an encounter with appetizing sweets or something savory, which ultimately leads to craving, are called imagery cues.

Understanding which food cues affect you is critical to losing weight. Learning to identify situations that lead to unnecessary eating or to overeating is a powerful way to control impulsive eating. By knowing your own set of food cues, you can avoid being in situations that make you overeat. As we continue with exercises in this regard, you will learn more about these cues.

✎ **Name ten cues that create cravings, in detail, and accurately. In the past month, how many times have you encountered these cues? For example:**

1. The smell of barbeque on my commute to work, 2 times
2. Watching my colleagues eating lunch: every day
3. Seeing processed meats in the fridge: 3 days
4. Buying fresh bread and cheese: 4 days
5. Watching a cooking show: every day
6. Talking about foods at a party: 1 day
7. The smell of pizza: 1 day
8. Seeing a cake behind the pastry showcase: 1 time
9. Seeing people who are buying processed meats and soda: 1 time
10. The smell of deep-fried potatoes: 3 days
11. 
12. 
13. 
14. 
15. 
16. 
17. 
18.

In the table below, situations associated with food cues are listed. Please read them carefully and think about them.

| Situation | Type of food cue |
|---|---|
| Encountering a chocolate bar on the kitchen table | Environmental |
| The sweet smell of a very good pastry | Environmental |
| Seeing food on the plate in front of you at a restaurant | Environmental |
| Seeing people who are eating at a party | Social |
| Thinking of last Saturday's dinner that was cooked by someone you love | Imagery |
| Seeing your friends eating in the workplace | Social |
| Going to a great bakery | Environmental |
| Remembering going to a highly rated restaurant | Imagery |
| Seeing your favorite food | Environmental |
| Smelling one of your favorite foods | Environmental |
| Seeing people who eat voraciously | Social |
| Being offered something delicious to eat | Social |

In this session, you are becoming familiar with the concept of food cues and their types. One of the most common reasons for being overweight is responding to the numerous food cues in one's environment. Confronting food cues in their surroundings happens to almost everyone, but why do some people respond more to these cues than other people? You might also ask why some people always seem to put themselves in situations that are likely to be associated with food cues.

In response, it should be noted that some people have brains that are more reactive to environmental, social, and imagery eating cues. If they see or taste food they like, they are unable to stop themselves from eating, and it's said that they are "reactive to cues". Reaction to cues among overweight people will be high, and when they encounter triggers and cues, their tendency to eat increases, leading them to eat more than they need.

On a scale from 0-10, how high would you rate your food cue reactivity?

In some "food cue reactive" people, eating even one bite of a food results in a severe craving and they are unable to stop eating. We call this "craving induced by a single bite". Some of the ways these people might describe themselves are:

1. Once I start eating, it's very hard to stop.
2. When I like something, if I eat even a few bites, I know I won't be able to stop.
3. If I taste my favorite food, I lose control and eat until it's gone.
4. Starting to eat a sample food will strongly stimulate my appetite.
5. The first bite of food will take away my power to cope with overeating.

The obese people may not have a strong craving before taking the first bite, but if they eat even a small amount, they can no longer stop, even if they're not hungry. This situation also represents a kind of high reactivity to food cues. Even a small bite acts as a cue and stimulates the person's appetite. But what causes some brains to be over-reactive to food cues?

There are many scientific explanations for it. Many studies have shown that people who have been deprived of food for a while for some reason, like those who experience strict diets, are usually more reactive to food cues than others, and their desire to eat is very high. For this reason, it's easy to understand why many people tend to eat more after a period of strict dieting and regain even more weight. There are also several other explanations for "high food cue reactivity" which we will discuss in the next chapters of the book.

One thing which may help you lose weight is to know more about yourself and your brain. Do you react to food cues and overeat? Or do you control your overeating when facing food cues? Do you usually try not to expose yourself to food cues, or are you happy to put yourself in the midst of food cues? Answering these questions helps you to know more about yourself because, in order to change our behavior and habits, we need this self-awareness. To achieve this understanding, please do the exercises of this step carefully.

Brain Box

# What's going on in your brain?[1]

Before reading this section, think about the following questions:

- How does the brain react to triggers?
- How does knowledge of the brain reduce eating induced by triggers?

Suppose you are in a room and there are several power switches on the wall next to the entrance. With one switch, you can turn on all the lights on the right side of the room, with the second, all the exterior lights will be turned on, and with the third, all the lights on the left side of the room can be turned on. All of these lights – based on their location – will be turned on and off by a specific switch. But how does this relate to the brain?

Our brain is like this room, and various parts of it are activated or lighted up by exposure to a trigger, while other parts are turned off. Areas of the brain that communicate with each other for specific purposes, and turn on or off simultaneously, are called Brain Networks, and the state of equilibrium between several interacting networks is called Brain States. But how were these brain networks discovered?

In a study[2], participants were asked to close their eyes for a few minutes and try not to think of anything. Along with this experience, they were placed inside a scanner and their brains were studied. When people were told to think of nothing, some areas of the brain were still activated, which is called the brain's Default Mode Network (DMN). Subsequently, the researchers asked people to talk about the topics which had come to their minds while they were in the scanner; some referred to environmental stimuli, such as an air-conditioner noise, a ringing telephone, or staff whispering. Other people reported thinking about themselves and their memories; for example, "This evening, I should get together with my sister," or about an argument that they'd had with a colleague the previous day. The third group was composed of people who reported increased attention to their bodies, and that they had become sensitive to minor changes that they did not normally notice. You might have experienced such a feeling while doing yoga or some other activity which requires little or no movement and having your head start to itch.

**But how are all these things and the brain's default network associated with eating?**
When we crave food, the brain's default mode network is activated. That is why on holidays, weekends, and when traveling, at which times people are usually less busy, the chances of having cravings and subsequently overeating will increase. The DMN is also the main source of creativity and ideation, so it becomes a problem when being faced with food.

**In contrast, when you do the following calculations, your brain is operating in a different network.**

12*2=         72÷9=          14+26=
3*14=         156÷12=        54+39=

In this case, another network in the brain is activated – the Executive Control Network (ECN). This network is related to the execution of individual schedules, and acts in opposition to the default network, just like a light that cannot be on and off at the same time. For example, if you're at home on Sunday and the smell of barbeque fills your brain, it's likely that your default mode network will be activated and you won't be able to focus on anything but that marvelous smell. Your mind goes blank, and your cravings are front and center. But as soon as your phone rings and someone gives you important news which preoccupies your mind, the executive control network is activated, which reduces your cravings without realizing it.

So how can we apply this information to losing weight or eating management? Normally, a person should be able to switch from the default mode network to the executive control network or vice versa, like shifting gears. If a person becomes distracted when confronting food triggers and cannot continue working until they've completely devoured the food. That person has a problem with the "switches" of these two networks. In the following steps, exercises will be introduced to strengthen these networks and their communication.

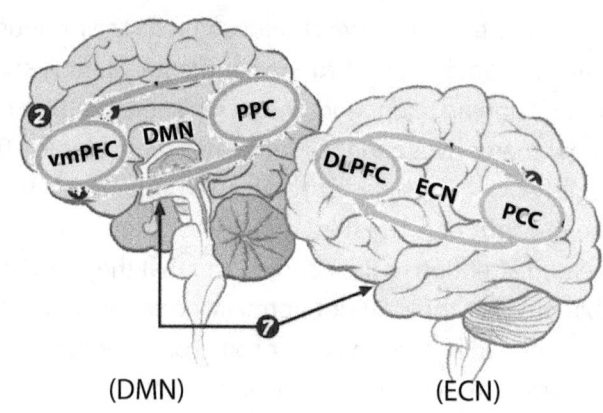

(DMN)　　　　　　　(ECN)
Default Mode Network　　Executive Control Network

Date: ..... / ..... / .....

## Your Own Footsteps on this Journey...

**1** So far, you've become familiar with the food cues and their types. Please consider your environment, social interactions, and mental imageries and fantasies regarding food. Identify your own food cues, and write them down in the table below. Also, in the third column, rate the level of your susceptibility to each cue on a scale from 0 to 10.

| Situation and cue | Type of cue | Induced craving (0 to 10) |
|---|---|---|
| At home, salted nuts in a bowl on the table | Environmental | 2 |

**2** In what situations do you find yourself experiencing "craving induced by a small bite"? Write down four items here:

1.
2.
3.
4.

**3** **What strategies do you have for dealing with eating which is induced by food cues?**

1. 
2. 
3. 
4. 

## Health note 5:

Studies show that obese people are 15% more likely to become fixated on food displayed in shop windows or in display cases, or to sit in front of people who are eating voraciously. Therefore, to prevent false appetites and food cravings, choose a place in restaurants so that the food display cases and people who are eating heartily are located behind you.

| Day | Monday | Tuesday | Wednesday | Thursday | Friday | Saturday | Sunday |
|---|---|---|---|---|---|---|---|
|  | / / | / / | / / | / / | / / | / / | / / |
| Weight | | | | | | | |
| | | | Daily Weight Table | | | | |

## Summary:

1. Identify your own triggers.
2. Continue to monitor your eating behaviors.
3. Distinguish between environmental, social and imagery triggers.
4. 

---

If you want to read more

1. Shannon D Donofry, Chelsea M Stillman, Kirk I Erickson, A review of the relationship between eating behavior, obesity and functional brain network organization, Social Cognitive and Affective Neuroscience, , nsz085, https://doi.org/10.1093/scan/nsz085

2. Mason, M. F., Norton, M. I., Van Horn, J. D., Wegner, D. M., Grafton, S. T., & Macrae, C. N. (2007). Wandering minds: the default network and stimulus-independent thought. Science, 315(5810), 393-395.

> **Step 6**  Date:  /  /

# Environmental Engineering

**How can you modify your environment in order to deal with overeating?**

So far, valuable information has been provided on overeating triggers, using which you can be more decisive in making decisions about changes in yourself and your environment. As you've seen, until this step, we did not want you to make changes in your current diet or follow a special diet. We just tried to improve your understanding of eating behavior, so that you could use this valuable knowledge to prepare yourself to change your behavior and modify your environment. From this step onwards, you will begin to make small changes in your life.

In the previous step, you became familiar with food cues. In this step, we will discuss the management of the cues, especially the environmental cues that give you cravings. One of the things that can reduce the effect of food cues on you is "environmental engineering," which includes changes to your living space, workplace, and even your daily route.

"General triggers" refer to a group of extrinsic stimuli, such as different types of sweets that commonly create cravings in the majority of individuals. In addition to general triggers, people also have their own "specific triggers". Hence, it is imperative that each individual recognizes their own specific triggers so that by identifying the triggers, they can seek and implement strategies to eliminate or mitigate their effects. For example, in some people, the presence of soft drinks in the refrigerator will make them take a drink whenever they open the door. If this is a problem for you, then it's best to avoid buying and keeping drinks in your home. The best way to engineer your environment is to change your buying patterns. Begin to make an effort to avoid buying high-calorie and unnecessary foods.

In recent decades, the expansion of large grocery stores and fast food places, while making it easier for people to buy food and meals, has also dramatically changed patterns of consumption. Having a wider variety of foods and snacks available has increased the purchase rate of high-calorie junk foods in our communities. Making unnecessary food purchases is one of the key reasons for being overweight and overeating which needs to be taken into consideration. The most important skills you need to learn are "how" and "where" to buy. Going to large stores leads many people into "unscheduled purchases," because you may be faced with a variety of new food. The layout and variety of these products are so attractive that even with your best efforts at resistance, you can hardly walk away from them. Keep in mind that every day, the owners of these large grocery stores are looking for new ways to attract more customers. That's why they use different methods to engage the buyer's mind, from offering a wide variety of snacks and foods at different prices, and appealing layouts, to incentives and rewards for bulk purchases. These are all means of increasing the customer's willingness to buy. But "unnecessary purchases," especially snacks, candy, cakes, processed meats, and other kinds of appetizing foods like sauces and pickles can be very detrimental to your path to recovery. Hence, as sellers use specific techniques to attract customers in order to achieve their goals, you must seek to counter their techniques and engineer your environment to avoid purchasing unnecessary high-calorie foods that usually have little nutritional value.

The goal of this step is to find strategies that can help you to reduce the effect of environmental food cues. Be aware that your food-dependent brain will try to encourage you to buy fatty, sweet, high-calorie items with harmful ingredients. For example, your brain says: "I'll buy some candy, but I won't eat any," "I'm buying this for others," "I'm buying it, but I'll only eat it for special occasions". Don't pay attention to these appealing justifications for sabotaging your surroundings and filling them with food cues. Instead, work hard on engineering your environment.

**Here are some tips for environmental engineering:**

1  Try to empty the fridge of unnecessary foods such as processed meats, all kinds of sauces, pickles, and snacks.

2  Keep your chocolate, candy, and nuts out of sight.

3  Be specific with your shopping list and resist the urge to make unscheduled purchases.

4  For a while, avoid buying and eating pickles and other condiments which might increase the level of craving.

5  When eating, feed yourself and your family just enough. Also, learn that if there's surplus food, it's OK to throw it away.

6  Change your daily route in such a way that you will not be confronted with shops and other places associated with eating (such as restaurants), especially places where you have a lot of enjoyable memories of eating.

7  When you leave the house, take with you whatever food you might need, so you won't be tempted to buy desserts, juices, or fast food.

8  Keep vegetables and fruits in the refrigerator washed and ready to eat.

9  Keep some nuts, dates, or other dried fruit in your desk drawer. That way, when you are under stress, you will be able to eat healthy foods.

10  Keep vegetables chopped and ready in the refrigerator and try to start your meals with a light salad.

As we said earlier, from this step onwards, we expect you to make changes in your behavior and your environment and be committed to maintaining those changes. So, from the tips mentioned in the environmental engineering list above, choose which of them you can do as a first step. Please select whichever strategy that will be easiest for you to implement, and work on it.

Make an agreement with yourself, according to which you will be obliged to do the things that are mentioned in the contents of the agreement, due to your commitment. Keep in mind that these agreements are designed to make you committed to your treatment plan. By making such agreements, the paths in which you must make changes will be specified.

**Brain Box**

# What's going on in your brain?

Before reading this section, think about the following question:

- Does the calculation of your caloric intake have an effect on weight loss?

Perhaps you've seen people who know everything about calories, and maybe even you yourself at certain times become one of these "weight watchers". For example, they know that 100 grams of grapes have 85 calories, one almond has 10 calories, and a glass of milk has 110 calories. But how effective are these calculations in losing weight?

One of the benefits of "weight watching" people claim is that by knowing the calorie amount of each food, they can control their behavior. Here, we encounter the familiar "control" word. If you want to interact with the things you've just learned, think about this: People say that when they don't have cravings, this plan works fine, but when they see a hamburger, it seems they lose their minds!

When people attempt to count calories, the brain's executive control network is activated and the control system does its job well, but as described in the previous step, when they have cravings, the network fails and the default network is activated instead. In the case of the calorie calculation method, they are relying on a system that fails during cravings, which may be one of the reasons for the failure of rigorous diets. In addition, these calculations literally use brainpower, and when the brain gets tired, the chances of overeating are increased. Nonetheless, there are many interpersonal differences and no general rules can apply to everyone.

We will continue our discussion with a baseball-related example. Baseball players have very high revenues, and the most important thing they need to know is when and where the ball will be thrown. But how does an outfielder catch a fly ball? By solving a series of complex differential equations? Or by doing something simpler?

In a study of baseball players, researchers found that a player does not have to estimate any of the variables necessary to calculate the ball's trajectory, including the initial angle and speed, spin, and direction of the wind, nor solve differential equations to calculate the point where the ball will land. Instead, they had a simple rule in their minds. Their gaze will guide them to that location without having to compute the exact spot, so they move at a speed that does not increase or decrease the angle between the eyes and ball and finally they catch the ball in the exact place; these simple rules which direct human action are called heuristics, a word from the Greek meaning "to discover".

Here are some examples of real-life heuristics that people use as a way to solve problems, or learn something, in economic and social fields; for example, in economics, we have this famous rule: "Don't put all your eggs in one basket!" which means that one should not concentrate all efforts and resources in one area as one could lose everything. Now we want to use these simple rules in terms of caloric intake. In fact, there are successful dieters who use a series of simple heuristic rules instead of complicated calorie calculations. For example, instead of calculating the calories of two peaches, a cucumber, and a banana, the dieter should get to this point that "eating fruit, in general, is good for health".

**Here are some examples of simple and valuable rules for your health model:**

1. Weigh every day and note it down on paper or on your mobile phone.
2. Do not eliminate any food group.
3. Have an appropriate response to hunger.
4. Cucumbers, lettuce, carrots, and other vegetables are great for health.
5. When you have done the same physical labor as a construction worker, then eat potatoes and rice as they do.

Date: ...... / ...... / ......

## Your Own Footsteps on this Journey...

**1 Identify five environmental triggers in your home that can be modified to help you reduce overeating.**

1.
2.
3.
4.
5.

**2** Name five environmental triggers at your work or place of education that can be modified to help you manage your overeating.

1. 
2. 
3. 
4. 
5. 
6. 
7. 

**3** In collaboration with your family, and paying more attention to your living environment and activities, list smart and effective strategies in the field of environmental engineering you could use to minimize your exposure to food cues.

1. 
2. 
3. 
4. 
5. 
6. 
7. 

**4** What are some of the problems with environmental engineering which you will probably encounter while trying to prevent overeating?

1. 
2. 
3. 
4. 
5. 
6. 
7.

**Please complete the agreement below for engineering your environment, and carry it through to the next step.**

> A small contract for environmental engineering:
>
> I _____ commit myself, based on the commitment and duty that I am giving to my weight loss, from today until reading the next step, to reduce overeating by utilizing the following environmental engineering strategies:
>
> Agreement date:           Your signature:

Have you bought a scale yet? Or have you put your scale in a suitable place so you can keep your eyes on it? Do you still feel bad about daily weighing? Are you still not registering your daily weight? Does the thought come to your mind, that "What are the benefits of weighing myself?" Creating new thoughts and behavior isn't easy, even getting used to a simple task like daily weighing. As mentioned in the first step, it's important to know that regular and stress-free weighing is an essential part of your overeating modification, and it is your key to success in this weight loss course.

> The risk of being overweight or obese increases by up to 33% in people who drink one or two hard beverages per day. Even drinking diet drinks is a problem, because the additives in those drinks increase appetite, so ultimately, even consumption of dietary drinks will cause obesity. Remember that other drinks aren't as healthy as water.
>
> Did you know that most beverages, not just tea and coffee, have caffeine, and for that reason, quitting them is hard?

| Day | Monday | Tuesday | Wednesday | Thursday | Friday | Saturday | Sunday |
|---|---|---|---|---|---|---|---|
|  | / / | / / | / / | / / | / / | / / | / / |
| Weight |  |  |  |  |  |  |  |

**Daily Weight Table**

## Summary:

1. The best way to manage the brain is to manage the input that the brain receives.
2. Environmental engineering means minimizing exposure to triggers.
3. The most effective source of willpower is environmental management.
4. Environmental engineering helps prevent willpower from wasting its limited capacity.
5.
6.
7.

---

If you want to read more

1. Pinto, A. M., Fava, J. L., Hoffmann, D. A., & Wing, R. R. (2013). Combining behavioral weight loss treatment and a commercial program: a randomized clinical trial. Obesity, 21(4), 673-680.

Step 7   Date: ..... / ..... / .....

# Emotional Triggers

**Why do I eat more when I'm not feeling well?**

First of all, we would like to congratulate you, as you signed your first agreement of behavioral modification in the previous step and decided to take an effective step for engineering your environment and taking action to make new changes. Following up on the topic of triggers, you will become familiar with the concept of "emotional triggers" in this step. Here's a preliminary definition of "feeling" or "emotion": "Emotion is a short and general reaction to an unexpected event with a pleasant or unpleasant emotional feeling like fear, anger, or love."

**In general, emotions have four basic components:**

1. **Trigger:** Generally, an environmental issue or event or a particular situation creates an emotional state.
2. **Cognitive interpretations:** The mind plays an important role in determining how we feel.
3. **Physiological changes:** The physiological arousal that accompanies the emotion: When a person has strong emotions, many bodily changes occur. For example, fear produces an increased heart rate, a rise in blood pressure, adrenaline secretions, etc.
4. **Nonverbal reactions:** Feelings often result in observable changes. For example, blushing or perspiring.

Let's learn more about the emotions by getting acquainted with three basic aspects, which can then be subdivided into many categories based on these three aspects:

1. **Severity:** The severity of experienced emotion, for example, severe rage.

2. **Level of Arousal:** The physiological response caused by emotion. For example, joy and anger have a high level of arousal, but calmness and sorrow have a low level of arousal.

3. **Weight:** The positivity or negativity of the emotion. For example, rage is negative, but joy is positive.

Emotional triggers are the emotional states which lead you to eat. It may have happened many times that you've eaten too much because of a stressor such as an exam. In this situation, eating is not a response to hunger; rather, eating makes you feel relaxed. One of the major problems for overweight people is eating while experiencing a negative or positive emotional state. These are referred to as "emotional triggers" which lead to the emotional states that give people cravings. Emotional triggers are divided into two categories: positive (such as joy) and negative (such as anger).

Emotions may affect your eating habits in a variety of ways. The different ways in which they influence you can be divided into four main categories:

1. **Creating hunger:** Emotional situations often create a sense of insecurity, and your body responds by trying to conserve energy. For example, stressful situations may result in a "fight or flight" response, creating hunger in order to conserve energy.

2. **Increasing sensitivity to cravings:** Negative emotional situations are often accompanied by a lack of pleasure, and because your brain needs pleasure, it may increase your sensitivity to cravings. In this way, the sight or thought of delicious food will greatly stimulate you.

3. **Creating cravings:** Emotional states (positive or negative) are often accompanied by a reconsolidation of eating memories. This communicating and reviewing of memories created by emotional states may make you crave foods.

4. **Impairing the brain's control system:** In emotional states, the energy needed for self-control is used up by the emotional conflict; therefore, one cannot properly control eating and cravings. People tend to eat in order to calm themselves down when experiencing negative emotional triggers

such as anxiety, loneliness, tension, anxiety, or sadness. Of course, overeating also occurs as a result of joy, as when you're at a wedding or on a vacation trip. In those cases, you indulge in eating as a result of the positive feelings you have.

**Think about these ten examples of emotional situations which can cause cravings:**

1. Conflicts with colleagues at work.
2. Disagreement with my spouse at home.
3. Worry when my child gets home late.
4. Being at home alone and feeling isolated.
5. Getting angry at something my spouse has done.
6. Feeling guilty about something I did to my mother.
7. Being ashamed of not handling my child well.
8. Going to a party and being embarrassed about my obesity.
9. Feeling that my rights have been violated.
10. Feeling that my spouse disregards me and doesn't love me enough.

Another important topic of discussion in emotional triggers is the premenstrual stage and menstruation in women. During their periods, women usually experience negative emotional states such as irritability, tension, restlessness, and disappointment. Other less severe emotional symptoms may also occur, such as stress, anxiety, insomnia, headache, tiredness, and increased emotional sensitivity. One of the strongest reactions to emotions during the period is cravings. Complications of overeating during menstruation or the premenstrual stage are common among many overweight women. Hence, they must be mindful of their cycle of menstruation while monitoring behavior and come up with plans to manage their negative feelings. Of course, it should be noted that similar emotional and mood changes during the month also occur for men, but with different degrees of intensity. Men, especially those who feel a lot of emotional volatility from one day to the next, should pay attention to this.

Another important point in this area is the proper understanding of the feeling of fatigue, and its difference from the sensation of hunger. Many people cannot distinguish between these two sensations. When they get tired, they think they're hungry and try eliminating their fatigue by eating. Perhaps because they have repeatedly experienced these two sensations at the same time, they respond in this way. Many people who are overweight usually start eating while they are tired and, as a result of the fatigue, cannot control their eating behavior. Therefore, another skill you need to learn is to differentiate between these two sensations. As mentioned previously, in some cases these two sensations can occur at the same time, but you should be able to differentiate between them. To do this, you can first relax before eating. Doing a series of stretching exercises can help with relaxation. Reducing fatigue when you're hungry can also help you eat less.

✎ **Think about two actual situations in the last weeks when you overate due to a combination of fatigue and hunger, and look at these examples that other people have come up with:**

*Situation 1:* : When I returned home at 8 pm, although I had eaten a meal at 6 o'clock with my colleagues and was full, I felt I had to eat something. I kept opening the refrigerator and getting something to eat.

*Situation 2:* : After cleaning the house, I was very tired and hungry. I ate some bread and cheese and felt full, but I still wanted to eat more. I opened the cabinet and ate everything inside it!

So far, food cues and emotional triggers have been introduced to you. In order to learn more about emotional triggers, you need to know how you behave in different emotional states and how much your cravings may increase. By doing the following exercises, you can get familiar with your different feelings and emotional triggers.

✎ **Look at this list of different emotions. The ability to name and describe emotions is the first step in recognizing them. Take note of every emotion's physical and behavioral symptoms in the examples here:**

| Emotion | Physical signs | Behavioral signs |
|---|---|---|
| Fear | Rapid heartbeat, paleness, trembling | Trying to escape from the frightening situation |
| Anger | Shaking hands and voice tremor, rapid heartbeat | Screaming/shouting, mistreating others |
| Grief | Loss of energy, insomnia | Feeling isolated, crying for no reason |
| Aversion | Rapid heartbeat, facial muscle contractions | Avoidance of others, destroying things |
| Joy | Increased heart rate, throwing shoulders back | Laughing, engaging more with friends |

| Emotion | Physical signs | Behavioral signs |
| --- | --- | --- |
| Surprise | Expansion of muscles around the eyes and mouth | Asking questions, scrutinizing the situation |
| Love | Rapid heartbeat, sweaty hands | Talking about the topic, doing the loved one's favorite things |
| Guilt | Feeling like there's something stuck in your throat | Drinking alcohol, excessive apologizing |
| Shame | Sweaty hands, paleness | Excessive sleeping, being hesitant |
| Regret | Scowling, being stoop-shouldered | Crying, re-interpreting memories to excuse the situation |
| Jealousy | Increased heart rate | Trying to defeat the rival, trying to emulate the behavior of that person |
| Rejection | Loss of energy | Defaming the other person, creating a plan for revenge |
| Distrust | Having a sensation of coolness inside the stomach | Avoidance of the person |
| Feeling impotent | Being stoop-shouldered, frowning | Pulling the rug out from under others, doing other things |
| Depression | Reduced desire to get things done | Crying, various types of misbehavior |
| Agitation | Increased heartbeat, having cold fingers | Avoidance of the topic, nail-biting |

**Brain Box**

# What's going on in your brain?

Before reading this next section, think about the following questions:

- How are the emotions related to eating generated by our brain?
- What changes do emotions cause in our brains which results in overeating?

When was the last time you had an emotional experience like sorrow or joy? What effect did it have on your appetite? Did it ruin your appetite? Or did you start eating, thinking this phrase over and over, "The only thing that calms me down is eating"? In fact, why do people react differently under extreme emotional conditions?

**Let's review the things that were mentioned in the previous pages:**

1. In unsuitable or negative conditions, the body feels insecure, and it starts to conserve energy, making you feel hungry and increasing your appetite – the kind of hunger that where you're apt to eat anything. Now, if we look at the historical origins of this issue, human beings have always faced stressors that threaten them with potential dangers, such as war, famine, illness, and so on. Dealing with these stressors required a lot of energy, which justified this eating behavior. What about the stressors most people experience now? Nowadays, the ultimate level of stress is generally limited to arguing with someone, getting a traffic ticket, being dismissed from work, or failing an exam, none of which are life-threatening. Therefore, the important question arises – do human beings still need this additional amount of energy to deal with these threats? Is survival still at risk? Perhaps the answer is that there is no rational justification for maintaining such overeating behavior in stressful situations within the present circumstances of our lives. Unfortunately, the human brain has not yet succeeded in changing this historical behavior.

2. Another reason for overeating during emotional situations is the brain's increased need for pleasure as part of crisis management. In negative emotional situations, the brain is designed to seek feelings of pleasure, and what is more easily attainable – and legal! – than eating? In such a situation, irritability resulting from cravings increases, and even the smallest thing which normally you would not mind can easily provoke you.

③ The next factor in most emotional states, whether positive or negative, is associated with the reconsolidation of eating memories. For example, consider a person who has eaten pizza whenever he felt good. Now, whenever he feels good, he craves pizza, because the feeling of well-being is associated with the good memory of eating it.

④ In the fourth mode, when your brain is in a highly emotional state, the control system is interrupted and self-control is almost impossible. For example, if an individual argues with his boss, the likelihood of being able to manage his eating behavior decreases.

Altogether, in emotional situations, we face four phenomena that differ from each other but may overlap and are diverse in different people. It is precisely for this reason that the experience of individuals in emotional situations can differ so much. Now, knowing this information, when is your eating influenced by emotional states? Which emotion has the most impact on your eating? Does your irritability increase or decrease? What is the intensity of your behavioral response?

Date: ...... / ...... / ......

## Your Own Footsteps on this Journey...

**1** Review your records from last month and identify the situations that led to overeating due to negative or positive emotional triggers:

**2** Carefully review your incidences of overeating due to emotional triggers and describe the type of overeating in those situations; for example: eating sweets, eating junk foods, eating ice cream, or eating heavy, greasy foods?

**3** When does this overeating due to emotional triggers make you feel good? Under what circumstances does it make you feel guilty and regretful?

**4** Please monitor your behavior and feelings from today until the upcoming session and record how you behaved in different emotional states, and to what degree you experienced cravings (as in the example below).

| How did you feel? | How did you behave because of this feeling? | Level of craving |
|---|---|---|
| Felt sad after getting a bad grade | Moody with parents, listened to sad songs, didn't participate in an evening party | 80/100 |

I _____ commit myself, based on the commitment and duty that I am giving to my weight loss, from today until reading the next step, to reduce overeating by these next environmental engineering strategies:

Agreement date: Your signature:

## Health note 7:

People who eat in response to tensions and stresses in life are thirteen times more likely to become overweight than those who don't. So, in stressful situations, it's better to go for a walk, take a shower, chew some gum, or drink a glass of cool water instead of eating.

The number of days marked in the table below indicates your commitment to change. It is not necessary to record your weight in this book every day. Just put a sheet of paper and a pencil near the scales and transfer the recorded weights to this book every few days.

| Day | Monday | Tuesday | Wednesday | Thursday | Friday | Saturday | Sunday |
|---|---|---|---|---|---|---|---|
| | / / | / / | / / | / / | / / | / / | / / |
| Weight | | | | | | | |

**Daily Weight Table**

## Summary:

1. Emotions consist of four components: 1) Trigger, 2) Cognitive interpretations, 3) Physiological changes, and 4) Nonverbal reactions.

2. Every emotion can be placed on a continuum according to these three perspectives: 1) Intensity of feeling, 2) Level of arousal, and 3) Weight.

3. Your eating behavior during emotional situations differs according to these four categories: 1) Creating hunger, 2) Increasing sensitivity to cravings, 3) Creating cravings, and 4) Impairing the brain's control system.

4. Understanding your emotions and their impact on your eating behavior is an important step in managing eating behavior.

5. Understanding your individual characteristics and personality traits and the relationship between emotions and your daily eating behaviors is important for weight loss.

6.

7.

**If you want to read more**

1. Adam, T. C., & Epel, E. S. (2007). Stress, eating and the reward system. Physiology & behavior, 91(4), 449-458.

2. Torres, S. J., & Nowson, C. A. (2007). Relationship between stress, eating behavior, and obesity. Nutrition, 23(11-12), 887-894.

3. Singh, M. (2014). Mood, food, and obesity. Frontiers in psychology, 5, 925.

4. Kukk, K., & Akkermann, K. (2017). Fluctuations in negative emotions predict binge eating both in women and men: An experience sampling study. Eating disorders, 25(1), 65-79.

5. Higgs, S., & Spetter, M. S. (2018). Cognitive control of eating: the role of memory in appetite and weight gain. Current obesity reports, 7(1), 50-59.

6. Ferrell, E. L., Watford, T. S., & Braden, A. (2020). Emotion regulation difficulties and impaired working memory interact to predict boredom emotional eating. Appetite, 144, 104450.

7. Smith, K. E., Mason, T. B., Crosby, R. D., Engel, S. G., & Wonderlich, S. A. (2019). A multimodal, naturalistic investigation of relationships between behavioral impulsivity, affect, and binge eating. Appetite, 136, 50-57.

8. Goldschmidt, A. B., Dickstein, D. P., MacNamara, A. E., Phan, K. L., O'Brien, S., Le Grange, D., ... & Keedy, S. (2018). A pilot study of neural correlates of loss of control eating in children with overweight/obesity: probing intermittent access to food as a means of eliciting disinhibited eating. Journal of pediatric psychology, 43(8), 846-855.

**Step 8**  Date:    /    /

# Eating for Emotion Regulation

**Why do we take advantage of overeating for emotion regulation?**

Emotions and feelings are an integral part of our lives and a sign of our vitality and play an important role in our decisions and behaviors. Pleasant feelings and emotions create positive energy, and unpleasant feelings and emotions create negative energy in us. It's hard to cope with negative and unpleasant feelings. Hence, people use various strategies to reduce them. For example, when they're experiencing feelings of sadness, they try to get rid of them by doing things like contacting friends or going for a walk. Others take up inappropriate behaviors such as smoking.

**Please think about a few negative emotions that you experienced last month. Here are some examples:**

1. Feeling rejection when my partner didn't care about what I was talking about.
2. Feeling inefficient when my child was acting up and I couldn't calm him down.
3. Feeling incapable when I didn't get a good score on my exam.
4. Feeling embarrassed when a teacher scoffed at my performance.
5. Feeling sad when I failed to finish something I started.
6. Feeling anxious and worried when I bounced a check.
7. Feeling jealous when my partner treated other people more respectfully than he/she treated me.
8. Feeling ashamed when everyone figured out that I was on diet again and would probably fail again.
9. 
10. 
11. 
12. 

Is it difficult to name and describe your past feelings? Were there times over the past few weeks you were feeling bad, but didn't know how to properly describe your feelings? Trying to increase emotional literacy by finding appropriate words to describe your feelings will help you to better understand them and manage them more appropriately. So when doing the exercises in this book, try to describe your feelings and emotions accurately.

Many people experience cravings when facing both positive and negative emotions. It seems that these people have chosen to eat for emotional management. Eating in such situations is usually extreme and associated with an inner compulsion that if they don't respond to their craving, they'll be quite upset.

For many people who are dependent on eating, a need to overeat is one of the side effects of negative emotions. That means that when they become angry or sad, an intense craving is created. For example, suppose that your spouse contacts you and announces in an apprehensible tone that he intends to talk to you when he comes home, but doesn't fully explain what the situation is. In this ambiguous situation, when you have to wait several hours until he comes home and shares the issue with you, you're likely to be nervous and angry, but you can only wait and try to calm yourself down. In such a situation, you may have intense cravings for food and eat angrily and rapidly. In this case, eating is serving as a method of stress reduction – you eat in order to avoid the stressful situation. To learn more about this response, you'll do the exercise on the next page.

✎ **Please review your overeating behaviors and think of examples of ways in which you used eating as an emotion regulator. Also, think about the effectiveness of eating for emotion regulation.**

1. Eating handfuls of nuts when I felt that my husband/wife didn't care about me.
2. Eating a whole bag of chips when I heard that my test score was bad.
3. Eating too much at a party when I felt that my wife/husband was looking at other men/women rather than at me.
4. Eating a whole pizza when I found out that my check had bounced.
5. Eating mac and cheese when I was tired of my wife's gossip about my mother.
6. Eating all the sweets and chocolates in the cupboard after my boss reprimanded me.
7. Eating a bagful of burgers when I was angry with my mother.
8. Eating lots of ice cream when I was tired and unable to cope with the kids.
9. 
10. 
11. 
12. 

As mentioned before, many people use eating as a way to manage their emotions. But why is eating used as an emotional control strategy? For the answer, we can look back at our earliest childhood memories. When we were afraid as infants, our mothers cuddled us and tried to calm us with breastfeeding. As a result, eating became not only an enjoyable activity but also a time of comfort when experiencing negative emotions. Eating, in addition to being enjoyable, diverts our attention effectively, albeit temporarily, away from negative emotions.

Overeating and being overweight are very common among people who use eating as a tool for emotional regulation and escape from negative feelings. This is especially hard if they have serious emotional problems. It's obvious that many people don't tend to overeat when their feelings are normal, but when they become sad or anxious or depressed, they behave impulsively or get agitated and may overeat. Perhaps you've heard somebody say (or even said yourself): "I wasn't fat at first, but I gradually gained weight after (a specific problem – for example, an emotional breakdown, financial crisis, separation, etc.) happened."

During negative situations, a tendency toward self-destruction or self-harm can increase. This can manifest in the form of high-risk sexual behaviors, overeating, or substance abuse, or in the simpler forms, such as excessive procrastination. In either case, these behaviors create enjoyment and can improve your mood even if only for a short time. As a result, your brain begins to feel that your emotions should be restored to normal at any cost, even the cost of fattening you up!

In situations where our mood is low, we naturally do not enjoy the events and activities that we've previously enjoyed, and our body lacks rewards. Therefore, we tend to adopt behaviors that create pleasure or make us feel rewarded, even if only for a moment. Many times, after a distressing event, you may have felt that you were not in the mood to carry out your plans or activities, and delaying them makes you feel a bit more relaxed. Unfortunately, this relaxation is short-term, so after a while, you actually feel worse because of the consequences of delaying your plans/activities.

This happens in relation to eating behaviors, or even sexual and addictive behaviors. Due to negative feelings, people tend to impulsively carry out harmful or high-risk activities for the experience. Afterwards, they feel calm for a moment, but soon their mood is worse than before and they become angry with themselves for behaving that way. They feel as if they don't really have the power to manage and control themselves, and this makes them even more distressed. If these behaviors are repeated over a long period of time, they become a lifestyle, the person grows accustomed to the behavior, and isn't even aware of the fact that he/she is hurting himself day by day. So what should be done?

The best thing is to examine our overeating-related moments and situations, and through looking at our past, **determine the starting point of our obesity and the occasions when it gets worse. Did things occur that were upsetting for me?** By answering this question, your self-knowledge increases.

Next, you have to answer this question, **"Is eating the only tool for emotional regulation?" Is there a good way to regulate emotions without these inappropriate strategies?** In the next session, we will discuss this important issue.

### Brain Box
# What's going on in your brain?
Before reading the next section, think about these questions:

- In situations where you're not happy, what do you do to make yourself feel better?
- Have there been any incidents in your personal life, resulting in excess weight?

Which eating-associated emotions have you experienced in the last week? How can you manage these feelings?

In the previous step, we discussed how emotions could stimulate the brain to eat in order to manage or adjust these emotions. But there are people for whom eating is the only way to regulate their emotions. What caused this to happen? Let us take a look at some common scenarios in a child's environment, perhaps we are not strangers to the scenes discussed below:

For example, a mother is walking with her child in a park when the child suddenly slips, hurts her hand, and starts crying. The mother, after cuddling the child and affirming her sense of security, buys her favorite snack in order to make her happy. The tears in her eyes begin to sparkle, and she stops crying.

In the next example, imagine a father who is alone with a child at home, but has a ton of work to complete by the end of the night. The child is restless and angrily throws all his toys around, screams, and wants to go to the playground, so the father gives him all the chips and donuts in the pantry to calm him down.

In the third scenario, consider working parents who leave their child with his grandmother during the day. The child becomes angry and scared due to the separation. This is where the "compassionate grandmother" competition starts. In order to win their grandson's heart, she makes a delicious lunch and buys lots of chocolates and snacks for him.

Well, what do all of the above scenarios have in common? Regardless of heritability, in all three scenarios, the child experiences negative emotions but lacks exposure to any appropriate emotion regulation skills, due to inappropriate conditions in their environment. Instead, he learns to eat whenever experiencing negative emotions in order to calm himself down. Children may also learn from their parents by observing this type of behavioral pattern. Parents are not excluded from this defective cycle and may also be victims of this kind of upbringing. This process occurs so frequently that even at an older age, we think the only thing that can make us feel good is eating, and we have an eating-dependent brain that is not readily willing to change.

The time has come to have a deep look inside ourselves and evaluate our experiences honestly: what effect, as spouses, parents, friends, and colleagues do we have on the eating habits of the people around us, in terms of tools for emotion regulation? For example, when seeing that your wife is distraught, how many times have you suggested that she go out to dinner with you in order to relieve her sorrow? Could you offer anything other than eating to make her feel better?

Think about that question and, without any judgment or concern, just consider your answer. Awareness is the first step in this treatment program. The next step is to increase emotional literacy, so we need to first understand the emotions, distinguish them from each other, describe them, and most importantly, recognize their power in a given situation. We also need to talk about them, because when you talk about something, your knowledge and control of that situation increase due to the visual image that is created in the brain's cortex; the neural mechanisms in this section will be discussed in more detail in the next step. Also, in the next steps, we will look at other healthy ways to regulate the emotions which don't involve eating.

Date: ....... / ....... / .......

## Your Own Footsteps on this Journey...

**1** Please think back carefully about situations recently where you used eating as a tool for regulating your emotions, and then fill in the table below using the following example:

| Event | Emotion | Your behavioral response |
|---|---|---|
| I had a discussion at work with my boss because of a delay in sending reports | 80 percent anger 20 percent frustration | Overeating and eating too quickly at lunch |

| Event | Emotion | Your behavioral response |
|-------|---------|--------------------------|
|       |         |                          |

**2** **What do you think of what you mentioned in the table above? What other methods could you have used to regulate your emotions? Please suggest a few.**

① 

② 

③ 

④ 

---

A small contract for environmental engineering:

I _____ commit myself, based on the commitment and duty that I am giving to my weight loss, from today until reading the next step, to reduce overeating by utilizing the following environmental engineering strategies:

Agreement date: _____        Your signature: _____

## Health note 8:

According to studies, people who sleep less than five hours a day suffer from abdominal obesity about two and a half times more than people who sleep more than eight hours. For better weight control, get at least seven hours of sleep per night, at a fixed time and on a routine. If your working conditions allow you to sleep for half an hour in the daytime, that can also be beneficial. But be careful! Oversleeping is also a factor in becoming overweight. By stopping overeting for a day, it will not have a significant impact on your weight. Generally, a change in our eating behavior, whether positive or negative, isn't reflected in our weight for about a week.

| Day | Monday | Tuesday | Wednesday | Thursday | Friday | Saturday | Sunday |
|---|---|---|---|---|---|---|---|
| | / / | / / | / / | / / | / / | / / | / / |
| Weight | | | | | | | |

**Daily Weight Table**

## Summary:

1. Emotion regulation is an important concept in changing your lifestyle and weight loss process.
2. Emotional awareness is a great help for emotional regulation.
3. If eating is your only tool for emotion regulation, it will result in obesity.
4. 
5. 
6. 

---

If you want to read more

1. Kelly, N. R., Tanofsky-Kraff, M., Vannucci, A., Ranzenhofer, L. M., Altschul, A. M., Schvey, N. A., ... & Yanovski, S. Z. (2016). Emotion dysregulation and loss-of-control eating in children and adolescents. Health Psychology, 35(10), 1110.

2. Czaja, J., Rief, W., & Hilbert, A. (2009). Emotion regulation and binge eating in children. International Journal of Eating Disorders, 42(4), 356-362.

3. Harrist, A. W., Hubbs-Tait, L., Topham, G. L., Shriver, L. H., & Page, M. C. (2013). Emotion regulation is related to children's emotional and external eating. Journal of Developmental & Behavioral Pediatrics, 34(8), 557-565.

4. Hansson, E., Daukantaité, D., & Johnsson, P. (2017). Disordered eating and emotion dysregulation among adolescents and their parents. BMC psychology, 5(1), 12.

**Step 9** Date: / /

# Emotion Regulation for Eating Management

**How can we overcome overeating by emotion regulation?**

"Regulating or managing emotions" means using thoughts, behaviors, or skills that empower people to have a better understanding of their emotions, such as recognizing when an emotion emerged, how emotions can be expressed, how these emotions can be used more effectively, and how to prevent potentially destructive effects. A large body of evidence proves that people who have emotion regulation skills are distinguished in every field of life and can improve their quality of life as well as their personal and social success. This ability is called Emotion Regulation or ER.

Psychologists believe negative or positive emotions in people are not caused by the event itself or another external factor, but rather the subjective appraisal and thoughts of the person about the event, incident, or external stimulus. In other words, whether we are happy or upset, following an event, depends on our analysis of the event. Therefore, an incident may suddenly emerge which will make us frantic, but if our perspective changes at the same time, it can make us laugh. The simplest examples you may have experienced are the jokes your friends make. Another example of these drastic emotional changes is a hidden camera show. In these programs, showrunners first create a disturbing situation, causing discomfort and creating negative emotions. Once the person begins to react to these negative emotions, the host tells him it's just a joke and that he's in front of a hidden camera. You can see the sudden change in emotions in his face. So what is really going on? How does a person who was very scared or sad a moment before suddenly start laughing? In fact, emotions can change very quickly, but before that can happen, your evaluation of the situation or thoughts about the event will need to change.

As you can see, the way in which we interpret an event is what makes it meaningful and creates either positive or negative emotions in us. You probably have experienced similar situations before.

Think about two emotional situations that could create two totally different feelings with two different thought patterns. Let's look at these examples to clarify the issue:

| Emotional situation | First thought | First feeling | Second thought | Second feeling |
|---|---|---|---|---|
| I was walking on the sidewalk and a person jostled me | Inconsiderate person – only thinking of himself! | anger | -he was distracted -he looked worried -maybe he was blind | Empathy compassion |
| I called my friend, but he didn't pick up the phone | I'm not important to him | sorrow | -he was busy - his mobile was on silent mode | less annoyance |

Given that our emotions can change so quickly, why is it so difficult to regulate them? Why can't we easily relieve our negative emotions or change the thoughts and self-judgment that make us feel bad? You need to realize that when a person is faced with an emotional situation, trying to drum up a good feeling or trying to be optimistic isn't enough to control one's emotions. As has been stated previously, the thoughts that a person has in such situations are extremely important, so one way to regulate emotions is to change our intellectual structures.

Of course, thought changing skills aren't easy and require training and practice. In general, there are two strategies for emotion regulation: 1) Strategies implemented prior to the occurrence of an emotional event (i.e., before an emotion comes about, to prevent it from occurring), 2) Strategies that are used to change or control emotions after an event occurs and emotions have arisen. The first strategy is more effective – that is, to change the environment in such a way that negative emotions don't occur. Of course, after getting emotional, strategies for changing our way of thinking and the re-interpretation of emotions are also effective, but the way people normally control their emotions isn't very effective. For example, if we try to control anger or love, but we don't change our thinking process about the subject, our feelings of anger or love will become more intense.

But how can these strategies be learned? You must first get familiar with your emotional states and be able to express them. Ways to regular emotions include, understanding, linguistic expression, and accurate analysis of emotions. The most effective way to strengthen the ability to identify and understand emotions is to increase your attentiveness to emotional states and be able to self-assess honestly. For example, by saying, "I'm happy when…" you'll gain a more accurate understanding of your emotional state. Consider your recent emotions and experiences - how well are you reacting? How often do these emotions come about? Monitor your emotional states. Monitoring makes it possible to identify your feelings at the moment they happen and helps you to have more objective reactions to these feelings.

Evidence shows that people who have emotional regulation skills are more successful in every area of life than those who don't. People whose emotional skills have been well developed are also happier and more efficient in their lives. On the other hand, those who cannot dominate their emotional lives are constantly engaged in internal and external conflicts, which reduces their ability to focus or think clearly. We don't intend to provide complete training techniques for emotion regulation in this step, rather, the goal is to familiarize you with the importance of emotion regulation, its practices, and the application of those practices in the management of overeating. If you are overweight due to emotional dysregulation, becoming aware of your problem, and seeking out effective emotion regulation techniques will initiate actions toward change! In the next steps of the book, we'll look at methods of emotion regulation.

✎ **Recall an event or situation that made you feel negative, and answer the following questions. (The following are examples.)**

Event/situation inducing negative emotions:
*My daughter is upset with my working outside of the home.*

What was your thought or evaluation of that event/situation?
*I'm not a good mother; I'm thinking only of my own personal development; I'm selfish.*

How did you feel and behave after that thought?
*I left work and came home early; I blamed myself and felt even worse.*

How can you evaluate the event/situation differently?
*A satisfied, empowered, successful, independent mother can be a good role model for her child. I just need to have better management of my time.*

How do you feel after changing your evaluation?
*I'm more relaxed and confident.*

✎ **Think of two negative emotions that are associated with overeating and suggest two effective ways to regulate those emotions other than eating. (See examples below.)**

| Negative emotion associated with overeating | Alternative ways to regulate emotion |
|---|---|
| Anger at the emotionally neglectful spouse | – Get help from a counselor<br>– Talk to your spouse<br>– Stay busy doing other things, like watching a movie or reading a book |
| Feeling of ineffectiveness in raising a child and being unable to deal with her stubbornness | – Study appropriate parenting techniques<br>– Accept your feelings of anger as a mother<br>– Accept your own defects as well as your child's faults<br>– Try to improve your parent-child relationship |

**Brain Box**

## What's going on in your brain?

Before reading this section, think about the following questions:

- How is it possible to regulate emotions with the help of the brain?
- What regions of the brain are involved in regulating emotions?

The human brain is a neuro-cognitive structure. In layman's terms, it can be said that it's like a computer with hardware (the cells and circuits inside the brain) and software (intra-brain processing). We call the hardware the "neural" section of the brain, and refer to the software as "cognition". This "software" section analyzes and evaluates the information to make decisions accordingly. We also need to know the brain well; that is, what are the various brain regions called and what are their functions. For example, you cannot drive a technically advanced car if you don't understand the functions of its various components, especially if you're wanting to do something specific with it, like off-roading! The need to recognize a system is essential for its optimal use and our brain is the most complex and important system we have. Unfortunately, most people have little information about it. It is our mission to make people more informed about the brain.

The human brain is a system that intakes information constantly. When a chocolate cake is in front of you and its image enters your brain, it traverses two main paths: One path enters the deep parts of the brain, while the other path enters the cerebral cortex (a thin gray layer covering the surface of the brain). Visual information enters the cerebral circuits from the back of the brain when they enter the cortex. As the information moves forward, it is being analyzed, so by the time the information reaches the lower part of the cortex (around the temporal lobe), we know what the object is! What color is it? What use does it have? And when the data enters the upper part of the brain (at the top of the head, the parietal lobe), we then know where the cake is, and whether it's large or small. In other words, when the information reaches the lower part of the brain, we know what the object is, and when it gets to the upper part of the brain, we know where it is!

In addition, information that goes to the temporal lobe is also connected to memory; for example, the sight of this chocolate cake brings up so many memories about this well-known dessert. Eventually, this information reaches the front of the brain. The front section (frontal lobe) is the high-function region. If you look at other animals, you can see how their brains have grown gradually through evolution. For example, a frog's brain is somewhat like the deep areas of the human brain, but more complex animals, such as reptiles and birds, have extra layers. This process has continued through to mammalian evolution. If you compare the human brain to that of a chimpanzee, you'll see that their brains are very similar. The main difference is the front section of the brain (the cerebral cortex), which is nearly one pound heavier in the human brain. There is a region in the prefrontal cortex of the brain that is specific to humans and does not exist in other primates. What is the function of this region, unique to humans?

The upper and peripheral areas of prefrontal cartex are central core of the executive control network which manage the deep areas of the brain. The lower area of prefrontal cortex is linked with language. Blessed with words, early humans became aware of their internal lives and developed the ability to talk about it. In other words, human beings, with the help of these advanced regions of the brain, can understand, analyze, and express their emotions, and have found ways to regulate them, something that other creatures are incapable of doing.

So, the next time you are facing a trigger which creates intense emotions, try to analyze its pathway in the brain and talk about your emotions, because the more you talk about an issue, the more control you have, thanks to the activity of the brain's prefrontal cortex.

Date: ...... / ...... / ......

## Your Own Footsteps on this Journey...

**1** In the previous exercises, you were asked to write down the situations that triggered negative emotions and cravings. In this exercise, first, write down your thoughts and feelings at the time you experience them. Next, change your thoughts and note the feeling associated with the new thoughts, as in the following example.

| Event | Before changing thoughts | | After changing thoughts | |
|---|---|---|---|---|
| | thought | feeling | thought | feeling |
| This week my son has an exam | He is always dependent on me to help him study. | anxiety | I can give him an opportunity to study independently. | calm |
| | I must always be concerned about him. | anxiety plus anger | I can trust his abilities. | joy |

**2** In the table below, please write down any negative feelings associated with overeating during past month, such as in this example, and think about effective ways to regulate your emotions instead of eating.

| negative emotions associated with overeating | emotion regulation used instead of eating |
|---|---|
| Felt rejected after being at a wedding party | Contacted close friends and set a date to go to the mountains |

## Health note 9:

"The bigger plate means more food, more calories, and more body fat." A study found that 98% of obese people use large plates.

Losing a large amount of weight quickly can be physiologically dangerous and generally results in quick rebounds. Our suggested rate of weight loss is about 1 to 2 pounds per week.

| Day | Monday | Tuesday | Wednesday | Thursday | Friday | Saturday | Sunday |
|---|---|---|---|---|---|---|---|
| | / / | / / | / / | / / | / / | / / | / / |
| Weight | | | | | | | |

**Daily Weight Table**

## Summary:

1. Using the right strategies for emotion regulation is closely related to success, satisfaction, and quality of life.

2. Life events and circumstances alone do not determine emotions.

3. Evaluation, interpretation, and self-commentaries on events that occur are the main building blocks of emotions.

4. Reforming beliefs and the way of processing situations is the best tool for emotion regulation.

5. Monitoring and reviewing which emotion regulation strategies are the most helpful and beneficial for you will help you to get a better idea of yourself and be more successful at regulating your emotions.

6.

7.

---

If you want to read more

1. Koechlin, E., Ody, C., & Kouneiher, F. (2003). The architecture of cognitive control in the human prefrontal cortex. Science, 302(5648), 1181-1185.

2. Rolls, E. T. (2005). Taste, olfactory, and food texture processing in the brain, and the control of food intake. Physiology & behavior, 85(1), 45-56.

3. Kolb, B., Mychasiuk, R., Muhammad, A., Li, Y., Frost, D. O., & Gibb, R. (2012). Experience and the developing prefrontal cortex. Proceedings of the National Academy of Sciences, 109(Supplement 2), 17186-17193.

Step 10    Date: ..... / ..... / .....

# Behavioral Activation and Self-Entertainment Skills

**How can we open up new ways to enjoy our lives?**

Having fun, such as participating in team sports, climbing, hiking with friends, going to a park, or watching a favorite movie, can make you happy. Happiness and vitality are valuable and useful elements of our lives, so much so that they have received special attention in psychological and religious teachings. Research has also shown that adults who participate in regular recreational activities are happier than those who do not. We should also note that recreational activities are the strongest sources of life satisfaction, and those who engage in them more frequently will have many more enjoyable experiences and happier lives. When you engage in activities that bring joy and happiness to you, a region in the brain called

the "reward center" is activated, raising a sense of satisfaction which can result in repeating that behavior. In other words, that activity serves as a reward and satisfies your brain's need for enjoyment.

That reward is the happiness, pleasure, and satisfaction that we experience following a particular behavior. For example, many times you've enjoyed eating certain foods and experienced pleasure and satisfaction from eating them, due to the activation of the reward center in your brain. Activation of this area will increase your desire to eat that food, in such a way that you will insist on having it. As a result, the behavior of consuming this food will be repeated again and again. Some foods such as sugar especially rapidly digested sugars, and greasy foods produce a substance in the brain called dopamine, which stimulates the reward center by causing an immediate exhilaration. That's why people like to eat sweets and fatty fried foods repeatedly. Interestingly, the reward area is not only activated by eating delicious food, but also when you are greeted with respect or are encouraged by your community for your successes; again, you will feel satisfied and pleased. In this circumstance, too, your reward area has been activated by dopamine. The stimulation of the reward area is like your brain saying, "That would be a good thing to do again; don't forget next time!" Naturally, we like to repeat things that give us enjoyment.

We all need rewards – they make our lives fresh and dynamic, and our life expectancy will actually increase with exposure. People use different means to enjoy life and reap the rewards they need, some of which are generally healthy (such as eating), and some of which are unhealthy (such as using drugs). Eating is an acceptable and legitimate part of enjoying life. But if eating becomes the only way of enjoying life, the result will be weight gain and illness. Therefore, we need to give attention to other types of rewards for fulfilling our needs. Rewards can be physical and tangible, like getting a prize in a competition, or emotional and intangible, such as the satisfaction of seeing a friend's smile of gratitude for the help you've given him or her.

One source of reward is doing recreational activities. Relaxation brings with it happiness and joy. It reduces irritability, and our sensitivity to and judgment about unpleasant issues will be less negative. Hence, having suitable leisure activities will help regulate negative emotions. Unfortunately, we are often less attentive to our everyday entertainment than we should be, and don't establish a routine for recreation, relying on inappropriate and harmful ways to meet our needs. In order to have a healthy life, we have to pay attention to our leisure time. In fact, recreation is a skill to be learned. First of all, we must acknowledge the need for it in our lives and establish a definite time for it. We need to think about different ways to have fun and create conditions to make fun happen. Regular recreation is a key factor in the activation of the energy-producing and motivating areas of your brain. If you gain pleasure through healthy recreation rather than from eating, your need for eating rewards will be reduced. That's why one of the most important factors we're examining in this weight loss treatment is to provide entertainment in your everyday life than eating. Having fun doesn't necessarily require a lot of money or free time. With a little contemplation and planning, you can make time to have fun and choose activities that won't cost too much. To learn more, please complete the assignments for this section.

**Think about activities that make you happy, other than eating.** These activities don't necessarily need to be things that create extreme pleasure. Activities that make you feel happy, satisfied, and relaxed are also important. One factor to consider in choosing an activity is feeling psychologically recharged and energized afterwards. You may also feel tired, but you should notice a significantly higher level of mental energy. For example, after a week of hard studying and sleep deprivation, you get an "A" on a difficult test and your professor and classmates admire you. In this situation, you feel tired physically, but your sense of satisfaction and happiness make you feel psychologically energetic. Let's take a look at some examples that people mentioned in treatment groups as being rewarding behaviors:

1. Watching children playing in a park
2. Solving a hard Sudoku puzzle
3. Mountain climbing and hiking
4. Playing with kids
5. Following correct procedures at their workplace
6. Going to the movies
7. Visiting a museum
8. Getting together with family and friends

Some of you may think that there are no good recreational facilities nearby in your city, or even in the whole country. The fact is that many forms of entertainment are available, but we often aren't actively seeking them out or creating appropriate recreational activities based on our budgets. Fun requires time and creativity! Many times, rather than devoting time to looking around ourselves or asking others for suggestions, we just gripe that there's "nothing to do," and fill our time by eating or lying around in front of the TV.

**To jump-start your recreational activities, keep in mind the following:**

① Put aside perfectionism. Typically, when people can't find something which brings them special pleasure, they abandon it. Find small pleasures in life. You can be sure that the benefit you gain from them will gradually make you feel better and you'll no longer need to eat excessively.

② Use available entertainment. Fantasies about luxurious activities which require special facilities will only make you feel worse. If you look around with an open mind, you'll be sure to find activities that can improve your mood without ruining your budget.

③ Be pragmatic. Plan your fun and find ways to force yourself to entertain. For example, ask friends or relatives to join you in an activity or buy movie, or concert, tickets in advance. In short, open yourself to fun, even though you might not be in a good mood when the time comes.

④ Handle the challenges. Evaluate your performance, anticipate potential barriers to the activity, and figure out how to overcome those obstacles.

⑤ Be creative. You don't have to settle for doing things that make others happy. Be creative and actively seek out things that are pleasurable and satisfying to you. Don't restrict yourself with a limited number of activities. Anything that makes you experience more happiness and satisfaction in life is worthwhile, and you need to give it a try!

**Brain Box**

## What's going on in your brain?

Before reading this section, think about the following questions:

- Can the stimulation of the brain, by food triggers, be reduced?
- What does the brain consider to be fun/enjoyable?

In previous sessions, the limbic system and its relationship to cravings were discussed, as well as ways to avoid cravings by reducing environmental triggers. Is it really possible to give up foods that have always been a source of pleasure? We can control what's in our homes, but not what's in other environments such as amusement parks, shops, the workplace, parties, etc., so whether we want it or not, we will sometimes be exposed to our favorite foods, or at least to their smells. So what is the right solution: escape, or resistance?

Realistically, we're not always going to be able to run away or resist, and asking every person around us to engage in environmental engineering is neither logical nor reasonable. The essential question is, "What should I do?" Can something be done to reduce the irritability of the subcortical areas of the brain? Even when there's a pizza in front of me, it doesn't have to stimulate me to eat!

In short, we need a way to reduce brain sensitivity to triggers, rather than attempting to prevent trigger exposure alone, in order to limit the power of environmental triggers. As we have said, the brain needs a certain amount of pleasure during the day. If eating triggers in the environment are extremely limited, yet a person only gets enjoyment by eating, then he/she will certainly be in trouble! We need to find the answers to these questions: Why does the brain need pleasure? And can we find another source for this pleasure?

If there is no pleasure, there won't be any learning. If we want to learn behavior through repetition, it should be accompanied by pleasure or reward. Another thing this pleasure system does is make us dependent. When we do something repeatedly and experience pleasure, the brain depends on it and doesn't see any potential harm. For example, imagine a person who has high blood cholesterol and loves steak. If we talk about the disadvantages of eating it, he will not only deny it but will be upset and angry with our remarks. This happens to those people whose only way of enjoying life is eating so that behavior constantly repeats itself.

When your brain pleasure inputs are low, such as when you're on a diet, your brain increases the sensitivity of the limbic system and the smallest things will be pleasant to you. For example, a stale cookie purchased 10 days ago may not be stimulating in a normal state, but for an individual with an overly sensitized system that has been deprived of food by a diet, it can be very stimulating. We need to create conditions in which eating won't be the only source of pleasure so that the pleasure center cannot be stimulated easily. But how can we boost the brain's pleasure center with things other than eating?

Through behavior modification, we learn a set of skills that can be enjoyable and also reduce the brain's sensitivity. There are few people who know how to enjoy a healthy life, people who have regular access to healthy pleasures, and proactively plan their week to enjoy them on a regular basis. In this step, review the following list of possible activities, and hopefully, at least some of them will meet the minimum requirements for your brain.

Date: ...... / ...... / ......

## Your Own Footsteps on this Journey...

**1** Below is a list of pleasant events and activities that might take place in anyone's life. Please read the list and indicate how often you engage in these activities. (Since some of these activities/events may not have happened to you, please imagine how you might react to them if they did). You can also mention your own experience.

| Row | Events | Never | Rarely | Occasionally | Frequently | Very Frequently |
|---|---|---|---|---|---|---|
| 1 | Participating in charity work | | | | | |
| 2 | Getting to know new people | | | | | |
| 3 | Talking about sports | | | | | |
| 4 | Listening to live music / attending a concert | | | | | |
| 5 | Planning trips or holidays | | | | | |
| 6 | Shopping for myself | | | | | |
| 7 | Doing arts & crafts such as painting, calligraphy, knitting, or photography | | | | | |
| 8 | Climbing with a group of friends | | | | | |
| 9 | Reading the Bible | | | | | |
| 10 | Playing badminton | | | | | |
| 11 | Changing home or room decor | | | | | |
| 12 | Reading a story or novel | | | | | |
| 13 | Going for a drive | | | | | |
| 14 | Breathing in fresh air | | | | | |
| 15 | Watching TV | | | | | |
| 16 | Talking to myself | | | | | |
| 17 | Going on a picnic | | | | | |
| 18 | Thinking about good things happening in the future | | | | | |
| 19 | Going on a pilgrimage | | | | | |
| 20 | Succeeding in doing a hard job | | | | | |
| 21 | Laughing | | | | | |
| 22 | Solving a puzzle | | | | | |
| 23 | Creating a puzzle | | | | | |
| 24 | Doing makeup or shaving | | | | | |

| Row | Events | Never | Rarely | Occasionally | Frequently | Very Frequently |
|---|---|---|---|---|---|---|
| 25 | | | | | | |
| 26 | | | | | | |

**2** Please make a complete list of all your recreational activities which do NOT include eating, and evaluate the level of pleasure you experience from each one from zero to 100. (See example.)

| Recreational activity | Level of pleasure (0 to 100) |
|---|---|
| Booking two tickets for Beyoncé's new concert Saturday night for myself and my partnes | 85 |

**3** Please select two practical/feasible activities from those listed on the previous page and make notes regarding the time, tools/equipment, and money you'll need to do them.

| Activity | Amount of time it will take | Tools/equipment needed | What it will cost |
|---|---|---|---|

You can create a table with all of your recreational activities

Choose one of the recreational activities on this page or the previous pages and arrange a time to do it one day this week.

> A small contract for environmental engineering:
>
> I _____ commit myself, based on the commitment and duty that I am giving to my weight loss, on (day/date) _____ to participate in (activity):
>
> Agreement date: _____  Your signature: _____

## Health note 10:

"Jump rope or walk and burn calory." Jump roping and walking are very simple and free cardiovascular exercises that help burn fat.

| Day | Monday | Tuesday | Wednesday | Thursday | Friday | Saturday | Sunday |
|---|---|---|---|---|---|---|---|
|  | / / | / / | / / | / / | / / | / / | / / |
| Weight | | | | | | | |

**Daily Weight Table**

## Summary:

1 Our brains naturally need pleasant experiences.

2 Behaviors that are accompanied by an experience of pleasure or, so-called reward, will be repeated by us in the future.

3 Rewarded and repeated behaviors lead to dependence on those behaviors.

4 In the absence of pleasure, the human brain becomes more sensitive to stimuli. Therefore, in the absence of pleasant experiences, the brain becomes more vulnerable to cravings.

5 If eating is the only source of pleasure and it is being repeated over time, the brain comes to depend on it and becomes vulnerable/sensitive to stimuli and cravings.

6

If you want to read more

1. Richards, J., Jiang, X., Kelly, P., Chau, J., Bauman, A., & Ding, D. (2015). Don't worry, be happy: cross-sectional associations between physical activity and happiness in 15 European countries. BMC public health, 15(1), 53.

2. Balish, S. M., Conacher, D., & Dithurbide, L. (2016). Sport and recreation are associated with happiness across countries. Research Quarterly for exercise and sport, 87(4), 382-388.

3. Nawijn, J., & Veenhoven, R. (2013). Happiness through leisure. In Positive leisure science (pp. 193-209). Springer, Dordrecht.

4. Berridge, K. C., Ho, C. Y., Richard, J. M., & DiFeliceantonio, A. G. (2010). The tempted brain eats: pleasure and desire circuits in obesity and eating disorders. Brain research, 1350, 43-64.

5. Iozzo P, Guiducci L, Guzzardi MA, Pagotto U. Brain PET imaging in obesity and food addiction: current evidence and hypothesis. Obes Facts. 2012;5(2):155-164. doi:10.1159/000338328

Step 11    Date: ...... / ...... / ......

# Social Values and Eating Behaviors

**How can we resist false social values about eating?**

In this session, we are going to address the social customs and beliefs about eating commonly used in our community. In our culture, there are good eating habits, such as taking small bites or chewing food well. Adhering to them can help reduce the problematic behaviors related to eating. In return, there are also false beliefs that could hurt us by fallowing them. Hence, paying attention to social values and customs is an important issue to consider in the treatment of weight loss, and adhering to customs and developing proper habits are important strategies in weight loss treatment.

✎ To find out more about this topic, read the following list of some common customs and common misconceptions about eating behaviors. Please read them and note which of these customs you are adhering to and which of these habits you have. Additionally, mention any other wrong customs, beliefs, and habits that come to mind.

| Right customs of eating | Wrong beliefs |
|---|---|
| Taking small bites. | In order to respect others, you should eat whatever you are offered. |
| Chewing food well. | Being chubby is temporary, and I can eat whatever I want. |
| Stopping before you are full. | The belly is a sign of wealth. |
| Not eating because of decreased appetite or desire. | Starting a diet or losing weight is for namby-pamby people. |
| Eating calmly and slowly. | Food without rice is not food! |
| My belly is not the rubbish bin; I won't eat the food that should be thrown away. | Eating extra food is a good way to avoid waste. |
| Eating before starvation. | Eating too much food will not hurt you. |
| Not talking while eating. | The host must eat until the last person gets up from the table. |
| Not wasting food. | The host should encourage the guest to try a little of everything. |
| Eating one kind of food at each meal. | The cooking of several types of food is a sign of respect for the guest. |

As you can see from some examples in the table above, in any culture, there can be many misconceptions about eating and being overweight, and you may also hold some of these beliefs. Unfortunately, many of these misconceptions that can lead to being overweight are unwittingly learned from our families, making them difficult to eliminate. Your family may commonly eat high-fat or starchy foods, or believe obesity is inherited and your family members will inevitably become or stay obese.

Some families encourage harmful eating habits, such as teaching their children to clean their plates, despite being full. You have heard this advice from parents many times who say to their children: "Eat, it's wasteful to throw away food." Sometimes parents who have eaten their own food will eat the rest of their children's food in order to reduce waste.

So, learn to put away extra food for another meal, or even throw it away! Eating too much food is actually wasting food, as well as damaging your own health. It does not matter if you put the extra food in the trash can or save it as fat in your body. Do not eat more than you need in order to reduce waste.

**Suppose you're eating a sandwich. You feel full and you don't want any more. What are the destructive thoughts and the appropriate thoughts in this situation?**

| | |
|---|---|
| **Destructive thought** | I've already paid for this sandwich. If I do not eat it all, it will be wasted. |
| **Appropriate thought** | True waste is when I eat something that my body doesn't need. |

Another form of social misconduct that leads to weight gain is thinking that you must eat anything offered to you, even if you don't want to. You might think that saying no would be rude! Many people who are overweight find that one of their problems is their inability to refuse eating when others insist. Keep in mind that while others, based on their own relationship to food might encourage overeating, you can consume as much as you need and avoid unnecessary eating. Avoid trying to read minds. Thinking that "If I do not eat, he is likely to become upset" is just your thought. Even if they insist you can say, "it's very delicious, but I've already had enough", you do not even need to explain yourself more. This way, you can cut out excess eating caused by social pressure.

**What are the disadvantages and advantages of saying yes or no to insistent offerings of eating? See the following examples.**

| Saying yes | |
|---|---|
| **Advantages** | **Disadvantages** |
| The host will be happy and satisfied. | Feeling guilty for eating too much. |
| Your interaction with the host will not be challenging. | Feeling angry with someone who has forced you to eat too much. |
| You will eat more delicious food. | Eating too much and getting out of the weight loss program. |

| Saying no | |
|---|---|
| **Advantages** | **Disadvantages** |
| Increased self-esteem for doing the right thing. | Upsetting the host. |
| Staying within your weight loss program. | Feeling embarrassed for declining. |

Another social behavior, or custom, common in our society is preparing a variety of foods at a party, in order to offer a diverse and colorful array. This can act as a trigger for overeating. You need to know that sitting at a table may cause you to follow the lead of those around and often eating is increased. So, until you learn to stop overeating, stay away from large parties and potlucks. If you must go, try to choose just one type of food and eat a small amount of it. Do not try to taste all the food, even a small bite, because tasting even a little may increase your urge to eat. One of the other social beliefs affecting weight is your family's point of view about fitness. If being overweight is looked down upon in your family, they may insist you lose weight and will support your weight-loss treatment. Sometimes family members seem to encourage fatness. Of course, this usually goes back to their own physical condition, perhaps they themselves are overweight and unconsciously dislike the idea of their spouse or child losing weight. Sometimes there are false beliefs in the family as well as "Chubby partners are kinder" or "Fat people are more fun" or "Children who cannot fit through the door are healthier!"

**Think a little about the beliefs that you and the people around you have about being overweight. In your opinion, what beliefs should be modified in you and your family about the overweight? Notice the beliefs people usually have in this regard.**

1. All of the food on your plate should be eaten.
2. Being on a diet at a party is disrespectful to the host.
3. We need to prepare several types of food to show the interest and respect of our guests.
4. Insisting others eat more food is a sign of our love for them.
5. If we love our partner, we should eat everything he/she makes.

It is very difficult to modify these beliefs, customs, or wrong behaviors. The first step in modifying these problems is becoming aware of their falseness and accepting the truth. In the next steps of this book, we will return to these cultural false justifications.

Brain Box
## What's going on in your brain?
Before reading this section, think about the following question:

- Is it possible to change the values and beliefs ruling the human brain?

Imagine a camera, that is set in its automatic mode, can capture high-quality photos in different situations, even if the person who uses it is not professional. But sometimes an error appears in the system and the photos are blurry. This is where point and click doesn't cut it, and the individual must manually adjust the settings to get the right shot. This can also have disadvantages, as one needs to know exactly what goes into the perfect shot; what is the shutter speed, what is the diaphragm, how is the depth of field set up, what is the focal point and so forth, which is no longer as easy as before. On the other hand, one has the benefit of getting to know the instructions and what the camera can do. It will be time-consuming the first time, but after repeating and learning something that the person did not know before, it will become automatic.

The brain is also this way, and its function is automatically based on values ranging from 200 to 300 years ago. While we believe that we can still have a high quality and healthy life based on these values, when illnesses and problems emerge, we must seek therapeutic and health-related solutions to recover. When we do this, we increase our body and brain knowledge to help us manage new situations. For example, perhaps due to the drought, famine, and other challenges of that period, the obesity of women was directly related to their fertility and their ability to feed the child, so it was an advantage. Over time, due to increasing the welfare, health, and progress of medical sciences and changes in the lifestyle such as reduced physical activity, urbanization, environmental pollution, and changes in food processing, obesity is no longer an advantage in pregnancy. The question is, should we continue to live by our predecessors' standards and see daily health-related problems in our families, or is it time to unsettle the stability of the brain and redefine our quality of life according to today's situation?

There is no doubt that the route will not be easy, and the brain considers this change as a threat to its survival and cannot easily let manipulate its positions. Also, people around you may sometimes support stability. So, we suggest to be patient, and do not accept any belief unless you are sure of the correctness of it based on scientific evidence!

Have patience, and repeat this sentence every day: "The situation has changed, and in the twenty-first century, we are not going to live according to the values of my ancestor's time".

Date: ...... / ...... / ......

## Your Own Footsteps on this Journey...

**1** **Please provide a list of the right and wrong customs, habits, and beliefs that you have about eating.**

| Wrong habits or beliefs which leads to overeating | Right habits or beliefs about my eating |
|---|---|
| A picnic without a big pot of mashed potatoes does not make sense! | I stop eating before I get too full. |

| Wrong habits or beliefs which leads to overeating | Right habits or beliefs about my eating |
|---|---|
|  |  |

**2** **Sign a small contract to modify a wrong habit about your eating:**

The contract for modifying wrong habits:

I          Commit myself, based on the commitment and, duty I have given to my weight loss; this week, I will set aside this wrong habit about my eating


Agreement date:                                          Your signature:

**3** **What justifications do you and people around you have for your overweight?**

① *I look cute chubby and everyone likes me and a little bit of extra fat is not a health hazard.*

②

③

**4** **What are the wrong cultures in your family that help your overeating?**

① *You cannot have a party without cream puffs!*

②

③

## Health note 11:

If it is possible, install a mirror on the wall in front of your dining table. One third of people who install mirrors reduce the amount they eat. Researchers believe that eating in front of the mirror reminds you of your weight loss goals. Studies even indicate looking at your body in the mirror regularly will help you to reduce eating.

The hardest part of losing weight is always the first 5 or 10 pounds, as others typically don't notice these first few pounds. From then on, the positive comments of others about your weight loss will help you continue this path.

| Day | Monday | Tuesday | Wednesday | Thursday | Friday | Saturday | Sunday |
|---|---|---|---|---|---|---|---|
| Weight | / / | / / | / / | / / | / / | / / | / / |

**Daily Weight Table**

## Summary:

1. Our social values about eating have been shaped by context over time and throughout history. These values have been tailored to our past economic and social conditions.

2. Today's life is different, so we need to change some of our rituals and values related to food.

3. Understanding these wrong values is the first step to correcting them.

4. Start with yourself and find new solutions to tackle social misconceptions about eating.

6.

7.

---

If you want to read more

1. Power, M. L., & Schulkin, J. (2013). The evolution of obesity. JHU Press.

Step 12    Date: ..... / ..... / .....

# Peer Pressure and Eating

**How to overcome overeating in family or friend's gatherings?**

As you remember, in Step 5, we became familiar with triggers. One of these triggers is social food cues, which includes family, friend, and colleague interactions. Research has shown that the influence of friends and relatives on obese people is greater than the impact of genetics and heredity. Wrong eating habits in the family, having overweight parents, especially obese mothers, having a gluttonous partner or friend can have a significant impact on our overeating. A study has shown that the influence of a group of friends can increase the likelihood of weight gain by about 75 percent and another study has shown that women who eat with four of their friends, on average, receive 150 kilocalories more per serving than women who eat with three of their friends. So, remember to base your parties and gatherings on things other than food! Sharing an office with a gluttonous colleague can be a disadvantage; on the other hand, a group of overweight colleagues, especially a group of women, who decide to start a weight loss program together, can encourage each other and continue on their weight loss journey.

The impact of family and friends on overeating is called "peer pressure", and can have a lot of impact on overeating for many people. This effect is either active and direct or inactive and indirect. For example, when a family member directly asks you to stop your weight loss program, or not to take part in weight loss treatment sessions, they will directly/actively prevent you from losing weight. Sometimes you do not realize this pressure directly or actively since it is hidden in other behaviors. If you don't notice these hidden obstacles, they can negatively impact your weight loss goals. For example, when you have a friend, colleague, or family member who is gluttonous or may even be obese, their presence might make it impossible to modify your environment and manage stimuli that make you overeat. The other step you need to take regarding your weight loss is managing and engineering your relationships. In the sixteenth step, we will go further into this kind of relational engineering.

Studies have shown that parental obesity, especially maternal obesity, directly affects childhood obesity; this effect is not necessarily due to genetic factors but due to the impact of a mother's behaviors on a child's weight.

**Please review your family and social relationships and write down the names and situations which would create a likely scenario to overeat. Use the following examples as a guide.**

| In relation to………. | In situations…………. | Type of impact |
|---|---|---|
| My colleagues | During breakfast | Inactive |
| My partner | During dinner | Active |
| My mother | In the weekend | active |
| My friends | On holidays | Inactive |
| Media like TV | Watching commercials | Inactive |
| Social media | Confronting pictures or describing foods | Inactive |
| Friends | Parties | Active |

| In relation to……….. | In situations………….. | Type of impact |

Please review the exercise above and find out the active and direct versus inactive and indirect relationships which lead to overeating?

As we said, peer or group pressure has an important role in weight gain. One of these groups is the family. Having gluttonous family members plays an important role in creating behavioral patterns and incorrect eating habits. In overweight families eating high-calorie foods is common and family activities often center around eating.

Overeating is a tempting activity for many, which is why we are heavily influenced by people around us. Whether your family members are overweight or not, they can have an impact on your motivation to start or continue the treatment. If they do not want to cooperate with you, controlling the environmental stimuli and engineering the environment will be very difficult for you. You may even face troubles with recreational activities. If you decide to lose weight, but your family members continue in their overeating behavior, they oppose your plans. You know eating is much more pleasurable if you have a companion while eating. Because of this, family members may ask you to stop your dieting and join them. This problem usually happens with married couples who both have weight problems, only one of them wants to lose weight, and his/her partner still wants to continue their overeating behavior.

So, in order to prevent these problems, it's best to behave very carefully and diplomatically and avoid arguing about this issue. Keep in mind that you need their support, not their aggravation. If you persuade them to either join you or support you, you may also change their behavior subtly. There is no need to deal with everything at once. You can continue eating with them, but instead of overeating, slow down your eating and fill up on salads and vegetables. When you do not want to eat a certain food, do not mention that it is high-calorie, but rather that you have no desire to eat it, or your taste in food has changed. Try to have an effective role in planning family gatherings and instead of opposing suggestions, offer suggestions that indirectly contribute to your weight loss program.

**If you are feeling overwhelmed by your family's attitudes, you should think twice before confronting the situation. Make a table like the one below for yourself. Get ready to face them by anticipating problematic situations.**

| Who is pressuring you to eat? | In what circumstances do you face this pressure? | What is the best answer you can give? |
| --- | --- | --- |
| My partner | At night, s/he comes home tired from work. | Before s/he arrives, prepare a colorful table of healthy foods such as fruit, fruit salad and welcome her/him with a cup of hot tea and a piece of biscuit. |
| My mother | When we go to their house on weekends with my wife. | From the day before, tell her that I want a chicken or how happy I would be if someone serves me pomegranates. |
| My friends | When we go to a party. | Talk to them about my problems and overcoming craving, and tell them how much I need their help. |
| My colleagues | When we have breakfast in the morning. | Tell them I cannot accompany them during breakfast. |

If your friends and family members don't have a habit of overeating, this can be a good opportunity to seek help from them during your weight loss program. For example, you can ask them to gently correct you when you overeat, or to help you notice and remove tempting foods from your environment. You can make plans to have fun with friends who don't have a habit of overeating. They probably have good suggestions for recreational activities that don't involve eating and can accompany you in such activities. For example, you may play games, watch movies, or go window shopping with them.

Always keep in mind that you must have a plan to deal with exposure to excessive pressure and be prepared to behave intelligently.

**Brain Box**

## What's going on in your brain?

Before reading this section, think about the following question:

- Does the brain really need as much energy as people think it does?

One of the interesting features of the brain is its economy. Allegedly, the human brain and its hundreds of billions of nerve cells, use only as much energy as a 100-watt lamp. This energy is much less than previously believed. The entire human body is similar, the amount of energy it needs is much less than what the general public believes. However, if you succumb to public opinion on this subject, and start to overeat, what will be the result?

Eating and thinking aren't as closely related as some people think. This belief that if we eat more, we will think more clearly is false. In fact, eating more than necessary only leads to excessive absorption and abdominal fat. Only 30% of what we eat is consumed by the brain. This excess is like mountain climbing with 25 pounds of apples, but you don't actually eat them! Imagine the amount of pressure you put on your body when you have excess body fat. In fact, when you consume 2,000 calories, you'll be much more energetic than when you consume 5,000 calories. Rather than doing healthy and beneficial work, the body must work to store these extra calories as fat, then carry that fat around.

Next time someone says, "It was ok to lose some weight, but now it's enough" or "There are circles under your eyes" rather than succumbing to this pressure and giving up your weight loss plans, pinch yourself at your waist. If you can feel fat between your fingers, be assured that your life is not at risk. Their concern may actually be due to the condition of their own brain. Brains are resistant to changes, and because their brains are accustomed to seeing you in a certain state, they are tempted to restore the status quo. For example, a mother and daughter started a plan to lose weight. The daughter makes a strong commitment and begins to lose weight. The mother, however, breaks her commitment and instead, begins to complain and discourage the daughter. The balance of her life has been changed. Perhaps, no one eats the meals she prepares or compliments her cooking anymore. The only way this good mother knows how to show her love is through her cooking, and her cooking is not wanted as much anymore. So unconsciously, without being aware of it herself, she tries every little trick to return to her previous lifestyle. In another example, imagine a husband who had been encouraging his wife to lose weight, but after the end of one session when changes are revealed in her eating style and food choice, he doesn't keep his word and tries to restore stability to their personal life by making comments such as "You look so weak!", "You are hurting your body!", "You are making a mistake", etc. If these situations arise in your own journey, try not to overreact. Just repeat to yourself that, "I am not hurting my body because I respond to hunger. I eat fresh fruits and vegetables, and I manage my cravings."

Date: ...... / ...... / ......

## Your Own Footsteps on this Journey...

**1** Please consider personal situations and social relationships that make you overeat and note how to deal with them in the table below.

| Situations or relationships that make you overeat | Coping strategies |
|---|---|
| My co-worker, who always has a chocolate bar on his desk | I asked him to place the chocolate bar in his desk drawer |
| | |

**2** Please refer to the list of recreational programs you have set for yourself, and choose the entertainment you can have with family members without eating food, and also check what facilities and planning are needed for that entertainment? Complete the requested information.

| The name of the recreational program | Tools and Equipment | Time | Implementation | Costs |
|---|---|---|---|---|
| | | | | |
| | | | | |
| | | | | |

**3** Please write a contract for this recreational program:

A small contract for environmental engineering:
I _____ Commit myself, based on the commitment and duty that I am given to my weight loss; On the day _____ this week




Agreement date:                    Your signature:

## Health note 12:

Ear Infection is also related to Obesity!
People who have ear infections mostly like oily and sweet tastes and the consumption of these oily and sweet foods is high, which also causes them to become overweight. So be careful of ear infection of yours and your children. Other diseases and infections can also increase your desire for sweet foods.

Human fat tissues secrete substances that lower your mood. Getting rid of even 100 grams of body fat is a very positive step forward to improve your mood and emotional well-being.

| Day | Monday | Tuesday | Wednesday | Thursday | Friday | Saturday | Sunday |
|---|---|---|---|---|---|---|---|
| Weight | / / | / / | / / | / / | / / | / / | / / |

**Daily Weight Table**

## Summary:

1. Pay close attention to the impact of family and friends on overeating behavior.
2. The belief that, 'In order to stay healthy, do not allow peer pressure prevail is a value.
3. Remember the situations when you often overeat because of the pressure of others. For each one, consider a solution and evaluate its effectiveness after implementing it.
4. 
5. 

If you want to read more

1. Faith, M. S., & Kral, T. V. (2006). Social environmental and genetic influences on obesity and obesity-promoting behaviors: fostering research integration. In Genes, behavior, and the social environment: Moving beyond the nature/nurture debate. National Academies Press (US).

2. Leahey, T. M., LaRose, J. G., Fava, J. L., & Wing, R. R. (2011). Social influences are associated with BMI and weight loss intentions in young adults. Obesity, 19(6), 1157-1162.

3. Raichle, M. E., & Gusnard, D. A. (2002). Appraising the brain's energy budget. Proceedings of the National Academy of Sciences of the United States of America, 99(16), 10237–10239. https://doi.org/10.1073/pnas.172399499

Step 13   Date: ...... / ...... / ......

# When Prevention is more Effective than Self-Control

**How can we reduce the need to control cravings by emphasizing prevention?**

In the third step, you became familiar with the concept of cravings. As we mentioned before, craving is "a strong desire to eat" which is much stronger than normal hunger. In this step, you will become more familiar with the concept of cravings and the ways to prevent them.

First, we want to know why people have cravings? And why do some people experience cravings more than others? If you remember, in previous sessions, you became familiar with the characteristics of food-dependent people and we said that some people are overweight because of their dependence on eating. In a group of food-dependent people, eating is not just a response to the need of hunger, but rather, they tend to eat in the presence of food cues, even when they are not hungry. In addition to this group, there are other people who have normal and controlled eating behavior in normal conditions, conditions in which there is no particular emotional state or experienced stress, but as soon as they become stressed

or experience negative or even positive feelings, they have cravings that are out of control. This feature is not only seen in overweight people, but also in people who are dependent on drugs or cigarettes, or those who experience emotional breakdowns, which can expose people to high-risk relationships. Research has shown that this behavior occurs in nearly 40 percent of overweight people. In other words, these people tend to have uncontrollable and extreme eating in a particular emotional state.

This behavior seems to be a mechanism used to manage emotions, especially negative emotions. Of course, this is not a good way to manage emotions and it can be replaced by better and more appropriate methods. However, in order to replace these behaviors, you must first learn more about yourself, to see if you are experiencing cravings and if so, under what conditions you experience them. Please do the following exercise carefully.

**Which of the following is true about you?**

- ☐ When I get angry, I eat more.
- ☐ When I get upset, I like to eat.
- ☐ When I overeat, I feel good.
- ☐ In stressful conditions, eating will calm me down.
- ☐ Food that smells good stimulates my appetite.
- ☐ When I go to a bakery, I'm unlikely to not buy anything.
- ☐ If there is cream puff in the fridge, it's hard not to eat it.
- ☐ When I see delicious food, I lose control.

If your answer to a number of these questions is positive, you can conclude that you are in the group of people who have experienced cravings in many situations. If you are familiar with cravings, you probably know that it is a powerful feeling that can hardly be controlled. Many people do not feel good about cravings because sometimes they feel so uncontrollable, the person sees no solution but to give in.

The story of craving can be likened to an avalanche: the avalanche is a huge mass of snow, which can begin as a small snowball, but as it moves downhill it grows bigger and bigger, triggering more snow, until it can't be controlled and causes massive damage. The primary movement of the avalanche requires a small stimulus, which leads to a big result. Cravings in many people are dependent on a small trigger or cue. Encountering tempting food, or a negative situation when you feel incapable of managing it, can be enough to trigger cravings. Trying to stop or control a craving requires a lot of energy, and sustaining this effort in the long-term, especially when you are tired, is very difficult and often unsuccessful. For example, many times you have decided not to eat sweets and put them aside. Perhaps you can control yourself for a few days, but very soon you will fail to control the cravings when confronted with delicious food, so you are repeatedly confronted with the bitter experience of failure. Frequent failures make you feel helpless against cravings and you begin to believe that a craving is a force you cannot overcome. You feel you have no choice but to surrender. You should not allow this feeling to happen to you. You need to know that when cravings are created and strengthened, it's hard to control them, but not impossible.

Now that you are more familiar with the concept of cravings, the question is what should be done about them? A craving is a feeling that many people experience, it is not unusual, and in fact, it's very natural. What matters is our behavior in response to cravings. Perhaps the difference between people who are overweight and those who do not face this problem is that, while both groups experience cravings, the severity of the experience is not the same.

One of the most important strategies in managing these cravings is to "prevent its onset." You are already familiar with eating triggers, so the best way to prevent a craving is to prevent the onset of food cues and emotional triggers. We emphasized on environmental engineering in several steps and asked you to create a list of precautions you can take in order to change your environment. You have even signed several contracts to modify your environment and have committed to do them. Please review the commitments you have made in this regard and answer the following questions:

- **How much success have you had in engineering your environment?**
- **What rewards did you consider for your success?**
- **In which aspects of environmental engineering have you failed?**
- **What are your barriers to implementing environmental engineering programs?**
- **What are your new programs for environmental engineering?**

In order to prevent cravings, in addition to environmental engineering, you should consider the prevention and management of emotional triggers. In the previous steps for managing emotions, two main solutions were proposed: 1) Strategies to prevent and regulate emotions; 2) paying attention to non-eating pleasures and finding ways to improve your vitality. As noted earlier, the more recreational activities people have the less negative they feel. One of the most effective ways to create happiness in life is to exercise daily. Exercise can motivate you to lose weight. Keep in mind that being physically active brings change to your life. Perhaps you've heard, "Being active gives you motivation and lack of activity makes you more stagnant." It is true, the more active you are, the more you desire to change. Starting to exercise with the goal of weight management is not as simple as it seems. Please refer to the section at the end of the book to use our suggested strategies for choosing and starting an exercise program. You have made a lot of decisions to make changes throughout this program, and these decisions all stem from your first decision, "I want to lose my weight." Now that you've reached the thirteenth session, we must congratulate you. You have passed an important part of the treatment course up to this step, and this is a great achievement. Hopefully, you have decided to continue your treatment and stay with us to achieve more success through working together.

**Please note the steps you have taken so far to change your lifestyle with the aim of preventing cravings and consider the examples that others have done in this direction.**

1. I'm shopping using a list.
2. I keep fresh-cut fruits and vegetables in the fridge.
3. I do not buy sausages or other processed meats.
4. I do not keep cookies and sweet drinks at home.
5. I send out the leftovers with the guests after any party.

**What else should you do to prevent the cravings in your life? I should:**

1. Ask my colleagues to stop encouraging me to have breakfast with them.
2. Ask my partner to cook healthier foods.
3. Not take sweets with me when visiting my friend's house.
4. Spend more time on recreational activities with no food involved.
5. Prepare and offer fruit for gatherings of friends.

Finally, remember that preventing a craving is easier and more effective than managing and controlling it in the next stages!

### Brain Box
# What's going on in your brain?

Before reading this section, think about the following questions:

- Do we use a particular formula to reach an ideal weight?
- How much can memories affect our eating behavior?

In this course, we do not have a concept of "Ideal Weight". For example, we do not say you have to do your best to reach 160 pounds! We do ask that you weigh yourself, regularly, and without judgment. Our goal will be clarified gradually during the next twelve steps as we empower you to manage your eating, and cravings, while liberating your brain from food dependency. For this reason, you will become more familiar with cravings in this section. An important aspect of cravings is food-related memories we have. How powerful are these memories? Memories of mom's homemade pies, high school snacks, Friday night mac and cheese, chocolate as a gift; memories which may be shared by many. You can also try to remember your own memories about food.

Interestingly, these mouthwatering tastes are not the same around the world. You learn this if you travel to other countries and get to know cultures of different nations. For example, raw shrimp, fish, and octopus a Korean might eat or fried frog legs enjoyed by a Chinese person may not be enjoyable to an American. If we look at the other side of the coin, some traditional American foods like clam chowder may not seem delicious to people of other nationalities. This exemplifies a fascinating concept: Our sense of deliciousness is different than other people, but sometimes we equate delicious with healthy or good.

When you look at different societies, you will not find this relationship between goodness and deliciousness; in fact, much of your perception of deliciousness comes from your childhood, and if these memories are emotionally charged, they have even a stronger effect. This means the difference between people, what they like, and how much they eat, goes back to their memories.

Imagine a plate of Texas Barbecue served for Mary and Sarah. Mary hasn't had this food before and she enjoys eating it and gets full, but Sarah from

Texas, after seeing it, remembers the childhood memories and starts to eat and cannot stop. She is so affected by the memories that she starts overeating, with memories acting as a trigger. In her emotional state, she eats more, leading to eventual discomfort.

Our memories about food can be divided into three categories: 1) Semantic: Texas Barbecue is delicious food, 2) Episodic: A memory that is associated with Texas Barbecue 3) Procedural: How can I mix Texas Barbecue with other ingredients to make it better? The next question is: can we change these memories?

There is a river called Lethe in Greek mythology, and those who wanted to erase their bad memories would drink from it. Currently, we do not have a river like that, but we have a very intelligent brain, a significant part of which deals with memories. Memories are a complex part of human existence. So far you have become familiar with their effects on eating behavior, but more importantly, there are techniques and methods to manage and rearrange memories related to eating that you will learn in the next steps.

Date: ...... / ...... / ......

## Your Own Footsteps on this Journey...

**1** Write down actions you can take in order to prevent cravings through curbing triggers. Also, express your ability to do that activity in terms of percentage.

| Prevention strategies of triggers | Feasibility |
|---|---|
| I refrain from buying chocolates and sweets because seeing them for me is a strong trigger to eat. | 95 |

**2** Write down suggestions that you can take into action in order to prevent cravings by curbing its emotional triggers. Also, express your ability to do that activity in terms of percentage.

| Prevention strategies of emotional triggers | Feasibility |
|---|---|
| During treatment, I am reducing my work pressure and its related stresses. | 60 |

Avoid bringing the pot to the table. A study has shown that bringing a pot of food to the table increases food consumption by about 35%.

During the past twelve steps, our emphasis was on your commitment to regular weighing without any negative feelings. Hopefully, after reading half of the book, you have made this important habit.

In the next steps of this book, we will address the physical activity issue. Please read the contents of the next two pages.

| Day | Monday | Tuesday | Wednesday | Thursday | Friday | Saturday | Sunday |
|---|---|---|---|---|---|---|---|
| Weight | / / | / / | / / | / / | / / | / / | / / |

Daily Weight Table

## Summary:

1. The best way to deal with a craving is to prevent it.

2. Environmental engineering is one of the most important techniques that will help you prevent cravings.

3. You need to have behavioral and recreational activities to make yourself less vulnerable to cravings. The more you use non-food pleasurable activities and resources, the fewer cravings you will have.

4. 

5. 

### 💡 Supplementary training: Exercise and management of overeating

Physical exercise is one of the first tactics that comes to mind for someone seeking to lose weight. However, many people who consider exercising, never actually do it, and those who start to exercise, except in rare cases, stop doing it after the first week. What is the problem and what is the solution? Does exercise truly lead to weight loss? Yes, aerobic exercises can be effective at burning fat. However, it's interesting to know that physical exercise, although it can maintain the reduced weight, in many occasions cannot directly result in serious weight loss. So why do so many people recommend exercise for weight loss? What is the main function of exercise in the management of overeating and being overweight? Physical exercise has seven important effects other than weight loss that are very effective in improving your health:

**❶ Exercise can change body composition by reducing fat and building muscle:** Although exercise reduces body fat mass, due to increased hunger and stimulation of muscle tissue, it does not generally result in serious weight loss. This shift in body composition from fat tissue to muscle tissue has many benefits. The fat tissue in the human body produces toxic substances that affect the human brain and cause anxiety and depression. Lowering fat tissue by doing exercise will improve your mental state and suppresses overeating induced by emotional triggers.

**❷ Exercise as a recreational activity unrelated to eating:** Exercise can answer your brain's need for pleasure and entertainment without eating a bite of food.

**❸ Exercise as an effective means of emotion regulation:** Exercise is an effective way to manage negative emotions that cause overeating. The impact of exercise on increasing the strength of areas of the brain responsible for emotion has been shown in various studies. Exercise also reduces the sensitivity of these deep regions to emotional stimuli.

④ **Effect of exercise in improving cognitive abilities:** Exercise improves brain functions such as attention. Strengthening the ability to pay attention will improve your ability to ignore the triggers of cravings and move away from them. Interestingly, recent studies have shown that the increased effectiveness of insulin in the brain after exercise helps prevent Alzheimer's.

⑤ **Exercise creates the opportunity to compensate overeating:** If in certain circumstances during your treatment you happened to overeat, having an opportunity to exercise will create the hope that you can undo what is done! This opportunity prevents the creation of a negative feeling and the continuation or recurrence of overeating.

⑥ **Strengthening the sense of efficiency and self-esteem:** Exercise creates a positive feeling of individual ability and improves self-efficacy. Other people also feel good about someone who is exercising regularly, because "a person who respects herself/himself will also be respectful to others."

⑦ **Exercise lengthens the life span by reducing the risk of heart attack, brain stroke, and diabetes:** In previous steps of this book, we mentioned that losing 10 percent of weight will reduce the likelihood of heart attack and brain stroke by half and if you add 30 minutes of daily exercise to this weight loss, the probability of these diseases will be reduced to about a quarter. It's interesting to note that regular exercise also significantly increases sexual performance. The most important and highly recommended advice for people with sexual dysfunction is to improve their diet and exercise regularly.

So, in conclusion, we need to know our specific goals before beginning exercise. It may not necessarily be possible to lose weight directly and rapidly using exercise, but ultimately, it is a factor in the continuation of reduced overeating, health, happiness, and improved quality of life along with longer life expectancy.

✎ **Why do many people despite understanding the positive effects, fail to begin an exercise routine?**

1. They think they'll wait until a day when they will be ready to do it.
2. They listen to their brain's excuses about hurting their knees or lacking time.
3. They don't have a precise program for creating the habit of exercise.
4. They can't get over their laziness.
5. They can't be flexible and modify their way of life.

Follow the book to find the right solution....

---

If you want to read more

1. Abarca, M. E., & Colby, J. R. (2016). Food memories seasoning the narratives of our lives.
2. Chan, S. C. (2010). Food, memories, and identities in Hong Kong. Identities: Global Studies in Culture and Power, 17(2-3), 204-227.
3. Lin, L., & Mao, P. C. (2015). Food for memories and culture–A content analysis study of food specialties and souvenirs. Journal of Hospitality and Tourism Management, 22, 19-29.

Step 14    Date:    /    /

# Craving Inhibition
**How to inhibit the induced cravings?**

So far, you have become familiar with the concept of cravings and their relationship with triggers, feelings, and emotions, especially negative emotions. In this step, we want to continue with cravings and introduce you to some methods of craving inhibition. Before that, we want to talk about the relationship between cravings and strict diets that result in deprivation.

Perhaps you have heard of, or experienced yourself, a major relapse after extreme dieting. Many people in this situation, when asked about the reason for their weight gain, say: "As soon as I stop dieting, I feel like I can't control myself anymore and I have a lot of food cravings." What happens to these people is quite clear. It seems that, in addition to medical causes, our psychological system does not tolerate severe deprivation and after a period of deprivation, the person faces intensified cravings. Research has shown people who want to control their weight begin eating more obsessively; for example, by counting calories every day, and exposing their body to severe deprivation, they are more likely to have strong food cravings. Therefore, one of the important points in preventing cravings is to not put yourself in a severe and prolonged deprivation in order to lose weight. If the failure of the diet is accompanied by a feeling of guilt, you will feel even stronger cravings, especially if you have experienced cravings in negative conditions. Here, we want to introduce you to a concept that plays an important role in breaking diets called the "vicious cycle." Cravings and eating induced by negative emotions is a two-way relationship. Emotions, especially negative ones, make you crave. On the other hand, when an overweight person begins to eat due to severe cravings, even though his negative emotions decrease temporarily, the onset of negative emotions may become worse after eating. Especially when a person is trying to lose weight and puts himself in a severe food deprivation, the cycle will happen more quickly and with greater power. Surrendering to a craving causes guilt as well as an inability to manage behavior. He blames himself and his self-confidence is diminished. Ultimately, this bad experience increases the intensity of cravings, such that the person feels he can no longer control his eating in any situation and will resort to eating a large quantity of food at once.

To clarify the concept of "vicious cycle," please read the following story:

Sarah is 24 years old and she is struggling with her weight. Her main problem is about her cravings for chocolate and cream puffs. She feels bad about her body and the pressure of her family and friends has forced her to lose weight. She has used various methods, but each time her diet lasts only for a short time. Recently, she found a vegetarian diet in a magazine, which claims that you can lose weight in a very short time. She decides to try this method, so she follows the diet for a few days, and generally deprives herself of sweets and chocolates. But one day, she returns home exhausted and without realizing it, eats chocolates from her candy dish. After this realization, she becomes angry, and this anger accompanies with a feeling of shame and guilt because she was not able to control herself.

As a result, Sarah begins to blame herself, causing her to feel even more negative. She cannot bear all this negative pressure; hence, she is looking for a way to reduce these bad feelings. The only way she knows how to deal with these negative emotions is eating. Suddenly she feels that she has no choice but to surrender. She says to herself: "I can never lose weight", "I cannot control this inner force," "I can not relax without eating", "I have to eat, just have to eat."

Eventually, she is faced with uncontrollable overeating behavior. In this situation, it does not even matter what she eats. She just feels her teeth and gullet cannot calm down a moment and they have to move constantly. Sarah goes to the fridge and consumes almost everything that is edible, with passion. Her negative emotions and uncontrolled eating continue in the next few days and exacerbate Sarah's weight problem.

✏️ **Do you experience guilt after eating induced by craving, like what happened to Sarah? Does this feeling of guilt make you overeat? Is there a vicious cycle of negative feelings and cravings in you too?**

1. You need to know that craving food is a completely normal feeling that exists in all humans. This feeling is slightly stronger in some people than others. The reason for this can be found in the early years of life. Currently, our problem is not finding the cause of this strength or weakness. Accepting the existence of cravings as a natural feature of the human body is the first step in managing it. Think about your own experience of cravings and remember that thinking, awareness, and expressing your own personal experiences about cravings and even sharing them with others will help you manage this natural feeling more effectively.

2. If your cravings are accompanied by feelings of weakness, incompetence, anxiety, worry, or sorrow, you should know that these emotions are due to your wrong craving-related beliefs. You need to accept that this feeling is natural and exists in everyone. Pay more attention to the existence of these craving-related feelings in yourself. Awareness of these feelings will help you manage them. You need to know that the existence of craving-related feelings will make you fail in craving inhibition.

3. If the presence of cravings makes you unable to control yourself and ultimately leads to overeating, do not worry, humans are generally not good at controlling their desires, and one instance of overeating is not going to make you obese. You must follow the teachings of the previous steps of this book and prevent future episodes of overeating by engineering your environment and inhibiting cravings. If you failed to control your cravings against delicious food in one instance, do not worry, enjoy the delicious food, but plan to not expose yourself to a similar situation again.

4. Do not escape from your cravings; instead, try to accept this natural human feeling, taste it, and check your body's response to it. Encountering a craving, accepting it, and feeling it without any negative emotions is one of the best methods for conscious management of cravings in the long term.

⑤ Craving does not necessarily mean eating. If you can separate a craving from the negative feelings associated with it and handle this natural human feeling without having a negative judgment, you'll be able to use methods to inhibit it.

**One of the best strategies for when a craving happens is the method of "distracting." Below is a list of things that can help you distract yourself. Read them carefully.**

- ☐ Reading the list of reasons for weight loss
- ☐ Calling a friend
- ☐ Staying away from food
- ☐ Going out of the house
- ☐ Drinking water or a low-calorie drink
- ☐ Sorting and organizing clothes
- ☐ Polishing nails
- ☐ Listening to music
- ☐ Watching a TV show
- ☐ Reading a newspaper or magazine

✎ **What are your suggestions for distracting yourself from cravings?**

An important way to succeed in "craving inhibition" is to have a predefined list of techniques and strategies you can use quickly when you have a craving without having to search for it. So be careful about doing this exercise. It's better to know your cravings may not be reduced rapidly by doing one activity. You might need to use several methods and learn to slowly diminish cravings over time.

**In the eighteenth step of this book, we will teach you more ways to inhibit cravings.**

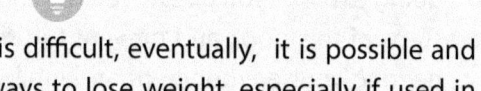

Although controlling a craving is difficult, eventually, it is possible and it is one of the most effective ways to lose weight, especially if used in combination with other methods.

Brain Box

# What's going on in your brain?

Before reading this section, think about the following questions:

- When confronted with delicious food, whose brain is more successful in controlling?

Dieters or non- dieters?

- Why do some people regain weight once they return to their usual eating pattern after going on a diet?

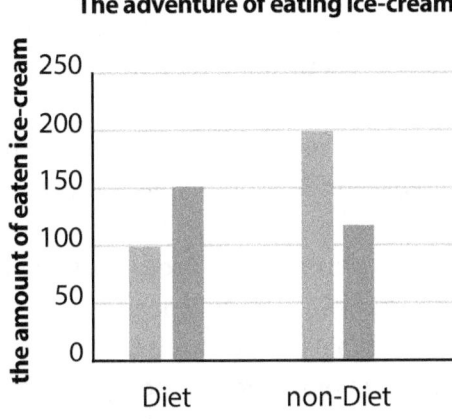

**The adventure of eating ice-cream**

In a study, subjects were classified into two groups. The first group were those who have gone on a diet and continuously controlled themselves and the second group were made of people who haven't gone on a diet until then. When the joint meeting ended, they have been told that ice-cream was going to be served outside the room and they could help themselves. Do you think those who were on a diet ate more, or those who weren't? The answer is clear: Those who weren't on a diet ate more and those who were on a diet controlled themselves; but in the second phase of this study, a group of different subjects was divided into two groups of dieting and non-dieting and a small change took place before they were served with ice-cream. The change was this: Before the end of the meeting, six small glasses of milkshakes (such as banana, strawberry, etc.) were given to participants and they were asked to taste them and see which ones are more delicious. Then they were asked to help themselves with ice-cream after the end of the session. In your opinion, what happened in this case?

Those who were not on a diet ate less than the previous time because they have lost their appetite, but those who were on a diet, when they ate the milkshake, they stimulated their appetite and ate more ice-cream than the non-diet group. Indeed, when people are on a diet and controlling themselves, everything goes well, but as soon as control is released in any way, like in the experiment with milkshake samples, people lose control and eat more. But what is the reason for this?

If you remember from previous sessions, we talked about the deep areas of the brain that are activated to create feelings, emotions, and desires. There is another area above the forehead that has control over its function and controls the deep areas of the brain. These two systems are always in conflict. For example, if a person sees a chocolate cake, his brain's deep areas are activated and forehead areas are deactivated, and he will probably crave. In some people, along with the activity of the deep areas, the activity of the forehead begins. In these people, there are conflicts between areas whether to eat or not. Some people when seeing food images, only the upper part of their brains start to activate so they can control eating behavior without any difficulty. So the first principle is that the human brain has systems that compete and each affects the other. It's like the presence of some people inside us, as one says, "Eat! It's really tasty," and the other says, "You'll be miserable! Don't eat!" Eventually, the outcome is determined by which inner voice wins. But the crucial point is that the conflict and interaction of these systems are not conscious until the moment we learn what's going on in our brains. The controls the brain performs are called brakes. Each person has a limited source of energy during the day that should be used optimally. On the other hand, the deep areas that are supposed to be controlled by the upper system are not the same and vary according to desire, emotion, and feeling. For example, a number of areas become activated when you get angry, some when you crave, and some other during sexual inclinations, while the control area is constant and has a steady and limited energy to control all of the deep areas of the brain and should act as one and control these areas. So people who go on regular diets should know that there is a limited source of inhibition, and when it is over, one cannot stop and will suffer from depletion and surrender to eating. If we look at a numerical example, the story becomes clearer: The energy of your control area is 100 units when you wake up in the morning. Imagine when you get out of the parking lot, you encounter the building manager and he gives you some advice that makes you irritated. Here, your control system is activated to manage your emotions, but its level of energy is reduced by 20 units. When you arrive at work, you notice that you have left your cellphone at home and you have an important appointment in an hour, and you become very angry and that reduces your energy by 50 units. When you return home at night, your wife is angry because you've forgotten to buy groceries. In this case, to prevent a fight, the control areas are activated which will take away another 30 units of your energy. At this point, your energy is depleted and in case of confronting a trigger like a pizza, you will have cravings. In a situation where control areas cannot cope, you are more likely to overeat. So, managing this energy is a skill that needs to be learned gradually, like a driver who knows how to press the gas pedal to drive safely, in order to avoid unnecessary braking. There are ways to increase the amount of energy stored in the forehead areas, which we will continue to discuss. There are also ways in which the stored energy in the brain can be refilled. At this stage, the first recommendation is to avoid events that drain this energy during the day, or at the very least, keep an eye on how much energy your brain has to control and, in the case of low energy, strictly avoid food triggers.

Date: ...... / ...... / ......

## Your Own Footsteps on this Journey...

**1** **Please provide a list of methods for distracting yourself and try to use them during a craving. Evaluate the effectiveness of each method from (0 = not effective to 10 = fully effective).**

| Activity | Effectiveness |
|---|---|
|   |   |

Keep this list with you available for review, so when you have a craving you can do the things that will help you in inhibit that craving.

**2** **Divide your surrounding networks into the following groups, in connection with your exercising:**

① **Opponents:** People who either consciously or unconsciously prevent you from exercising regularly.

② **Encouraging:** People who encourage you to do regular exercise in any condition.

③ **Comrade:** People who can exercise with you and help you to continue the exercise.

④ **Indifferent:** People who do not play a positive or negative role in this regard.

Having a network of friends who have a regular exercise program can be the most important factor in starting and continuing exercise. At the same time, the presence of an oppositional or indifferent person can make you never start exercising. So, to succeed on this path, increase your awareness about your networks and try to increase the number of encouraging people around you. You can measure your friend's attitude about exercising by stating, "I'm going to the park in the morning and I'm exercising for half an hour." Reactions like, "What patience you have!", "You know the pollen count is high", "Can you do the thing you promised me, instead of exercising this week?", "You know there are better ways to exercise", or "Walking is bad for your knees" are bad signs. Even indifference, shown by changing the topic of discussion is a bad sign. Try to reinforce the presence of people around you who will tell you: "Good for you, I'll come too" or "I congratulate you on your strong will!"

"Tie a ribbon around your waist"

One of the successful weight control methods popular in France is to tie a ribbon around your waist. French women tie a thin ribbon around their waists under their clothes, so if they eat too much, their belly will press against the ribbon to remind them to stay in shape.

| Day | Monday | Tuesday | Wednesday | Thursday | Friday | Saturday | Sunday |
|---|---|---|---|---|---|---|---|
|  | / / | / / | / / | / / | / / | / / | / / |
| Weight |  |  |  |  |  |  |  |

Daily Weight Table

## Summary:

1. Craving is a powerful and natural phenomenon in a human's life.
2. The first step to face cravings is observation and monitoring.
3. The second step is to accept cravings as a natural fact.
4. The third step is flexibility and adaptability.
5. Negative emotions and thoughts which accompany cravings, such as a feeling of guilt, put the person in a vicious cycle.
6. You can have a craving but not respond to it.
7. One of the most important strategies for controlling cravings is to prevent it from growing too fast in intensity. To do this, you should use attention distraction methods toward cravings.
8.

### Supplementary training: Features of suitable exercise to manage overeating

If you do not have a serious regular exercise routine so far, you need to know that in order to start this activity successfully, you need to choose exercises that have the following characteristics:

1. **Being fun:** Your exercise program should be enjoyable to satisfy your need for recreation; it should help you in regulating emotions and eventually, become a habit that will last you a lifetime. Accordingly, we strongly recommend that any selected exercise be performed with pleasure and without pressure, at least for the first three months. For example, if your chosen exercise is running in the park, just walk in the park and enjoy the scenery for the first few months. Insisting on running and sweating and putting the body under the pressure will unconsciously keep you from continuing.

2. **Availability:** The availability of facilities and adequate space is one of the requirements of the exercise. If you plan to go to a specific gym that is far away from your home or office, your chance of success in continuing throughout your life will be reduced.

3. **Reasonable fees:** Paying a monthly fee for using a sports facility or gym increases your commitment to do it, but this cost should be reasonable and the continuation of payment for the rest of your life, shouldn't put you under serious financial pressure.

- **Not making decisions during the exercise:** If your exercise involves making multiple decisions, it may be difficult for you to continue to perform it. For example, going to a fitness club without having a predetermined schedule or supervising coach will force you to make various decisions. For example, you have to decide what device to use today, what power should it have, what should be the next device, or how long should you stay in the gym. The existence of a predetermined program contributes to the continuity of the exercise. The exercises that you need to complete the entire track once you started are ideal for this, for example, walking around a park at a steady pace is an exercise that you can do without having to make a lot of decisions.
5. **Daily constant schedule:** The more you exercise at a specific time and as a regular daily program, the longer it will last for a lifetime. For example, people who leave the house every day at 6 o'clock, and after half an hour walking around the park near their workplace, go to work, are more likely to continue this activity. It's even advisable to continue this daily program on weekends or on trips. After a long period of active implementation of a daily program, you will see that it's hard to stop the program, and our main goal in exercising is, "creating conditions that you cannot (or don't want to) stop your exercise even for a day."
6. **Avoid injury and overexertion in exercise:** Never forget that the ultimate goal of exercise is your health and happiness. So, if you choose an exercise that would cause joint pain, extreme tiredness, and/or muscular discomfort, according to our criteria in this book, you are unlikely to continue doing it.
7. **Compete with yourself:** Registering your exercise activity and seeing your progress over time can encourage you to continue. This registration and progress review in any sport can have different ways; For example, people walking can record a timestamp for a route. Reducing the elapsed time step by step will give you more motivation to continue. But you need to be careful not "to get carried away" because speeding up and putting too much pressure on yourself can become a major factor in your failure.
8. **The positive effect of having a coach:** Having an experienced coach who arranges your exercise program can be effective, but remember to tell him of your goals and make sure that he can help you reach those goals. Do not forget you are not trying to prepare yourself for a sporting event!
9. **Commitment to Exercise:** Commitment to the exercise program and the

importance of being involved with it, is a prerequisite for your success in sustaining this behavior. You should not give your exercise time to any other activity, even if this activity is a meeting with the president himself.

**10 Do not forget the purpose of the exercise:** Once again, review the exercise goals in the book's previous step, and do not forget the purpose of the exercise. If after a month of exercising, you didn't lose weight, do not get upset. You are certainly moving forward to your goals and improving your health. So, continue on your path.

Now, according to the teachings in this part of the book, make a list of activities with the above features. Which of these activities do you want to start?

1.
2.
3.
4.

---

If you want to read more

1. FCampos, P. F. (2004). The obesity myth: Why America's obsession with weight is hazardous to your health. Penguin.
2. Pritchard, M. E. (2008). Diet is a 4-letter word: What can be done about America's unhealthy obsession with weight?. International Journal of Psychology Research.
3. LPolivy, J., & Herman, C. P. (2020). Overeating in Restrained and Unrestrained Eaters. Frontiers in nutrition, 7, 30. https://doi.org/10.3389/fnut.2020.00030
4. Herman, C. P., Polivy, J., & Esses, V. M. (1987). The illusion of counter-regulation. Appetite, 9(3), 161-169.
5. Polivy, J., Herman, C. P., Hackett, R., & Kuleshnyk, I. (1986). The effects of self-attention and public attention on eating in restrained and unrestrained subjects. Journal of personality and social psychology, 50(6), 1253.
6. Schölvinck, M. L., Howarth, C., & Attwell, D. (2008). The cortical energy needed for conscious perception. Neuroimage, 40(4), 1460-1468.

Step 15    Date: ..... / ..... /

# Cravings Reappraisal

**Looking at cravings in another way!**

Up to this step, we tried to get you familiar with cravings, triggers, and strategies that help you prevent them or reduce their severity. In this step, we want to concentrate on strategies to reduce the severity of cravings. One of the strategies we discussed in the previous step was shifting attention. Now, in order to assess your experience using this strategy, complete the following exercise.

✎ **Please review your behavior during a craving and see which strategies can help you more. Take a look at the list below and see which strategies you can use:**

| Cause of cravings | Description of eating behavior induced by cravings | Applied strategy | Result |
| --- | --- | --- | --- |
| Anger | Arguing with my wife during lunch made me incapable of controlling myself while eating, so I overate and felt that if I do not manage myself, I would end up eating throughout the night. | I left the table very quickly, and I started to organize my wardrobe. | As I was arranging the wardrobe for an hour, my anger decreased, and I didn't have as many cravings as before. |
| Smell of food | There is a famous Pizzeria near our home. Once I was coming back home very tired and I could not resist my cravings so I bought a pizza and ate it. | I changed my route on the way back home. I actually avoided the smell of pizza. | Since the cravings were not provoked by the smell of pizza, I did not even think about it. |
| Having snacks in the cabinet | I was bored at home and had nothing to do. I rummaged the cabinets and tried different snacks. | I called my friend and chatted for a while. | When the phone call was over, my wife and kids came back home and I totally forgot what I was planning to eat. |
| Feeling lonely | On my way home, I felt lonely, there was no one to help me cope, love me, or care about me. I went to a fast-food restaurant and ordered a pizza and french fries to make myself happy. | I checked Instagram and other online shopping sites to look for a perfect curtain for my new apartment. I gave the food to a homeless man. | Because I had found a new way to make myself happy, I was content with myself and I had given the food to someone who needed it more than I did. After that my cravings were completely resolved. |

**Remember this chart again:**

Another way to reduce the intensity of cravings is to change the content of craving-induced thoughts. Imagine being in a place where there is an appetizing stimulant to eat (like in a restaurant) and food that's very tempting for you. You pay attention to that food and a good impression of it will form in your mind (It looks delicious or it's made of the best ingredients). Following these thoughts, your appetite will increase, and you will eat it. If we want to use this strategy to reduce the intensity of cravings, we must change the content of our thoughts. For example, in the example above, instead of thinking that the food is cooked from the best quality meat and therefore it's delicious, we can remember that it's made with a lot of fat and the good smell is because of the fat. Fat also accumulates in our veins, leading to heart disease. In order to become more familiar with the strategy of changing the content of thoughts, please complete the following exercise.

✎ **Please complete the following exercises to get to know more about your thoughts and how to change their content when dealing with triggers:**

| Trigger | Thoughts that have come to your mind | Change thought content |
|---|---|---|
| Eating a spoonful of ice-cream | This ice-cream is really delicious and I cannot ignore it and I have to eat it up. | This ice-cream is made up of high-fat cream, sugar, and other ingredients that are very harmful to health. |
| Seeing a chocolate cake in the fridge | I worked hard all day; I have the right to take a break. I will start to get back on the diet tomorrow. | I do not need to intake these extra calories to relieve my fatigue. Perhaps a hot shower can relax me more than anything else. |
| My daughter asked me to buy her chips | I want to lose weight and this is my problem, not hers. | I am responsible as a mother for my health and the health of my child, and should be careful about developing my child's eating habits. |

| Trigger | Thoughts that have come to your mind | Change thought content |
|---|---|---|
| Hearing about a neighbor's death, who was in fact very fit and athletic. | This world is not worth getting so riled up about food. No matter what I do, I will get sick. So, it's better not to deprive myself of the joy of eating. | This is the justification of a dependent brain. All studies show that obesity is one of the major causes of many diseases and reduces the quality of life. To have a better life I need to take care of myself. |

Using shifting attention strategies and changing the content of craving-induced thoughts can reduce the intensity of our cravings. As mentioned in the previous step, another strategy is to increase your awareness of cravings. That is when you face cravings despite your efforts to reduce them, accept that having a craving is a part of human nature. Do not be afraid of your cravings or seek to escape them, this is not the answer to your problems. You have to face your cravings. Try to see them without any negative or positive judgment, accept them, and ultimately you will overcome them. You need to understand your experiences during a craving. For example, how do you feel in your stomach? how does your mouth feel? When you observe your craving like this, you reduce its power as your knowledge becomes greater. The unknown seems very powerful and uncontrollable, but when you accept your cravings and try to feel them wholeheartedly, you will become more familiar with them and it will decrease your fear of your cravings and the power they seem to have over you.

 **Answer the following questions.**

- ✓ **What was the last time you've had cravings? What feelings did you experience?**
- ✓ **What strategies could you use to prevent having cravings by eliminating the triggers from the environment (environmental engineering)?**
- ✓ **What were your solutions to shift your attention from triggers and induced cravings?**

**✓ What strategies could you use to reduce your cravings by doing a reappraisal?**

In general, in terms of cravings, you have to consider two important issues: First, a craving is like a snowball, it's small in shape and grows bigger and bigger gradually through your thoughts. You can prevent cravings from getting bigger and becoming uncontrollable with the solutions you've learned so far. The second issue is responding to cravings, which often puts the person in a vicious cycle leading to eating, feeling guilty, and eating more. Getting in this vicious cycle will not help your progress, it will discourage you from continuing the path by creating a sense of frustration and failure.

So far, we have offered you various ways to manage your cravings. Sometimes, despite all these efforts, inhibiting still fails. In fact, resistance to cravings is a tough task and takes a lot of energy. By reviewing the strategies mentioned, you will find that we do not want you to let cravings happen, and then resist them, because this is very difficult and frustrating. If you couldn't manage your cravings with all of these strategies, you'd better accept them instead of confronting them.

If you sometimes lose control of your cravings, do not blame yourself and do not feel guilty. Negative feelings are not only unhelpful, but can actually intensify the problem. Thinking of yourself as all-powerful in controlling cravings is a false belief as well. It is better to learn acceptance and forgive our mistakes, without surrendering to cravings. Craving-management is a skill; you can manage cravings by doing exercises and repeating them. Despite all the skills you can learn, you must accept your mistakes and forgive your overeating and try to increase your ability to prevent cravings.

**Brain Box**

## What's going on in your brain?

Before reading this section, think about the following questions:

- How can we change the memories of food?
- Can we control cravings by changing the way of processing information?

Imagine sitting on a bus. At the next station, a father with his three mischievous children get on the bus. One of them is a bit of a handful, the other screams, and the little one harasses the old man sitting next to the window. The father is silent and does not reprimand them. How are you feeling and what comes to your mind? You'll probably be angry and you think what an inconsiderate dad he is!

After a few minutes, the father who was sitting next to you says, "Excuse me, the children are very loud. We were at the hospital and their mother who had cancer passed away. I do not know how to give them the news and I'm still confused." How do you feel at this moment, and what thoughts come to your mind? What happened? What made you have such a different experience? The triggers were the same. In both cases, there were playful kids who were noisy. What changed your reaction? In fact, the way you process the information has changed which is related to the brain's saliency network. What does this network do?

Suppose there is a chocolate cake in front of you. The brain begins to analyze before you make the decision to eat it or not. How tasty would it be? Is high-quality cacao used? Should I eat it or not? What if I eat? How is it prepared? By answering these questions, the brain examines the importance of the subject. At this time, the saliency network is active. Another important task of this network is the balance between default mode and executive control networks and the determination of which network to use based on the response given by the individual. What are the techniques you can use to change the function of this network and manage your cravings?

Following the example above, how much liquid oil do you need to make a cake?

At least one glass! Are you ready to take a glass of oil and drink it? Or if it is solid, eat it with a spoon? But if you were asked to eat the whole cake, you would do that easily. If you've ever gone to a bakery shop that supplies pastry ingredients, you know that the cream that they use is not the cream we know, but a pastry cream mixed with vegetable oil or palm oil, which you are undoubtedly familiar with the disadvantages of. Perhaps you remember the controversial news about the use of palm oil in some factories. But why don't you have the same reaction to the use of palm oil here? The next issue is the use of paraffin wax in chocolate, yes you heard it right, paraffin wax! If it is not used, chocolate would not stay in shape. Are you ready to mix your chocolate with paraffin, the main ingredient of the candle, and then eat it? Or, in another case, you may have experienced leaving bread out of the fridge for several days, and you've seen mold. If you keep the cake out of the fridge for a month, maybe it will become dry, but it's impossible to mold. This is because of the antifungal powder that bakeries use in large quantities, while the substance is toxic and only a small amount of use is suggested. By knowing all of this, if you were given a chocolate cake right now, will you still enjoy it?

What we've done above is called reappraisal, which is used to change the processing mode and is strongly related to memory. As we mentioned in the previous step, the individual's memory is powerful and it won't surrender easily to this technique but the key point is repeating. Whenever you come across a trigger (here it is a chocolate cake), all the good memories you have with it are activated. But before the memories are resumed in the hippocampus area, and gained more power, to control the salient network, and cause a storm in the deep areas of the brain, like limbic area, you will break this vicious cycle with reappraisal, and you will come up with new nasty memories to replace old memories and erase them. But how?

Studies over the past few years show that recalling and remembering a memory, like what you did in the previous steps, makes these memories unstable in the brain for a short time. If you create a new memory using reappraisal or behavioral activation, then this new memory will gradually stand next to the old strong memory, and if this happens, a new memory will be able to replace the old memory. This is called memory reconsolidation. Consider a person who, based on his experiences of childhood, whenever he felt bad, he began eating snacks, like chips. Since he started this program he now reviews his memories when he begins to feel bad. As a result, these memories will be available more easily. At the same time, the person starts using the reappraisal to define the situation and the trigger differently, then he also learns to use a new healthy skill; for example, he says, "whenever I feel bad, I can watch a movie I have already prepared." By repeating this method continuously, the person will be able to stabilize his condition in the long run.

Date: ...... / ...... / ......

## Your Own Footsteps on this Journey...

Shifting attention and reappraisal are two effective ways of reducing cravings. Find examples of situations in your life that lead to cravings and find solutions using these two basic strategies to manage cravings. Rate the effectiveness of your solution from zero to 10.

| Trigger | Boosting Thoughts | Strategy | Effectiveness |
|---|---|---|---|
| Looking at your favorite pastry | How delightful it will be if I buy sweets! | In many bakeries, they use solid fats that are very harmful. | 4 |

💡 **Supplementary training: With the description set out in the previous pages, we have provided you with an appropriate exercise. Let's give you an example of a successful exercise that is generally associated with a high degree of continuity.**

❶ "A quick walk every day before rush hours, for example, from 6 to 6:30 AM on a circular path around a beautiful park, with a length of about 1.5 to 2 miles for 30 minutes, even on holidays." Of course, this is convenient for those who are early birds, and the same example can be true from 10 to 10:30 PM, for people who enjoy exercising in the evening. It should be emphasized that everyone should actively find his or her own ideal exercise according to their work and lifestyle. Just do not forget that your exercise routine should be very enjoyable and not stressful, at least for the first three months in order to ensure its continuity.

❷ According to the fourteenth step training and your experience in the meantime, what kind of exercises can provide you with the ideal conditions for the exercise to become a lifetime habit? Be careful to choose the right sport to be both enjoyable and attainable (at any time and any place). Do not wait for someone to accompany you to start a sport. Do not condition yourself to exercise only under specific circumstances. If you choose sports that have a challenging aspect, the sense of success in that challenging situation is also an attractive bonus for your brain.

Eat less, eat healthier, and exercise more. This is the key to your health.

| Day | Monday | Tuesday | Wednesday | Thursday | Friday | Saturday | Sunday |
|---|---|---|---|---|---|---|---|
|  | / / | / / | / / | / / | / / | / / | / / |
| Weight | | | | | | | |

Daily Weight Table

## Summary:

1. Your thoughts will strengthen your cravings.
2. Replacing destructive thoughts by constructive thoughts will prevent cravings from getting uncontrollable.
3. Food is not attractive or unattractive on its own.
4. Our memories and beliefs about certain foods make them attractive or unattractive.
5. Changing and correcting beliefs about different foods will affect the level of cravings.
6. 
7. 

---

If you want to read more

1. Hon T, Das RK, Kamboj SK. The effects of cognitive reappraisal following retrieval-procedures designed to destabilize alcohol memories in high-risk drinkers. Psychopharmacology (Berl). 2016;233(5):851-861. doi:10.1007/s00213-015-4164-y

2. Ecker, B., Ticic, R., & Hulley, L. (2012). Unlocking the emotional brain: Eliminating symptoms at their roots using memory reconsolidation. Routledge.

3. Lee, J. L., Nader, K., & Schiller, D. (2017). An update on memory reconsolidation updating. Trends in cognitive sciences, 21(7), 531-545.

4. Lane, R. D., Ryan, L., Nadel, L., & Greenberg, L. (2015). Memory reconsolidation, emotional arousal, and the process of change in psychotherapy: New insights from brain science. Behavioral and Brain Sciences, 38.

5. Ahn, Hyeon Min & Kim, Shin & Hwang, In & Jeong, Ji & Kim, Hyun-Taek & Hamann, Stephan & Kim, Sang. (2013). The effect of cognitive reappraisal on long-term emotional experience and emotional memory. Journal of neuropsychology. 9. 10.1111/jnp.12035.

Step 16    Date: ..... / ..... / .....

# Relationship Engineering

**How to modify relationships that cause overeating?**

Up to this step, you have become familiar with various topics of overeating management and losing weight, and one of the important topics that we have been addressing several times was the topic of "social triggers." In the twelfth step, we fully discussed the role of family, friends, and colleagues in overeating, and we asked you to identify relationships with people who cause you to overeat and take the necessary steps to reduce social triggers. "Relationship Engineering" is one of the important issues that should be fully addressed in your weight loss program. As mentioned earlier, eating is a tempting activity and the presence of gourmand people around you can screw up your treatment program, especially if these people are members of your family because you cannot leave them or limit your relationship.

Before going into details of the relationship topic, we ask you to consider an important subject. The vital factor in eating and communication is your memories. Many people start overeating while facing food because their memories deliberately or unknowingly lead them to do so. Whenever your memories are accompanied by emotional states, they will be strengthened and guide

your behavior. When you go back through your past and review the memories associated with your emotional eating, you'll find out how these memories and emotions lead you toward eating. Create new memories by eating in the presence of family and friends will help you in the process of losing weight. For example, eating healthy foods, rather than junk food, alongside your mother or child will help reframe the experience of eating with family as a healthy habit.

We need to first classify our relationships before we can come up with solutions for the engineering of relationships. When you are in a weight loss program, some relationships may be problematic for your progress. These relationships are divided into two categories of active and inactive. Earlier in the group pressure discussion, you have come to know this category of relationships. Active problematic relationships are relationships in which people consciously or unconsciously force you to eat more and reject your weight loss program. For example, a husband who prevents his wife from engineering her environment and ridding their home of the foods that are triggering, because he does not want to make these sacrifices.

In the inactive problematic relationship, you may be in touch with people who indirectly urge you to eat, for example, friends who go to eat pizza regularly (empowering inactive problematic relationship). On the other hand, some relationships stimulate your overeating, like having a gourmand colleague who constantly eats sweets in front of you (provocative inactive problematic relationship). One of the steps you must take in your relationship engineering is to identify the type of relationship. You can see all these kinds of problematic relationships in your interaction with your family, friends, and colleagues. The more exposure you have to the problematic relation, and the more influential this person is in your life, the harder your environmental engineering practices will be.

In contrast to the problematic relationships, other relationships are helpful to weight loss programs. These people often help or guide your weight loss journey. Some of these constructive relationships are "encouraging," like a mother who encourages her daughter to attend a weight loss treatment. Other constructive relationships are "modeling" relationships. These are people who you look up to as models of health and fitness and as your weight loss journey goes along you may find that you have naturally become much like your inspirational friends. The third type of constructive relationship makes you "empowered" to lose weight, like a friend who accompanies you in sports or recreational programs. Finally, some of your friends, family members, or colleagues will have no particular effect (either positive or negative) on your weight loss program. Now that you are familiar with a variety of relationships, think about your relationships and respond to the exercises below.

Create a table like the one below and write down the names of your family members. Consider your relationship with them, then estimate the category into which the relationship falls. Use the following examples to fill out your table.

| Names of your family members | Problematic relationship | | Constructive relationships | | | Effect less |
| --- | --- | --- | --- | --- | --- | --- |
| | Active | Inactive | Active | Inactive | | |
| | Empowering | Provocative | Encouraging | Modelling | Empowering | |
| Wife husband (Sara/ Mike) | | | Every week I declare my weight loss S/he encourages me. | | | |
| Child (Daniel) | | I'm being irritated when he eats. | | | | |
| Mother (Amelia) | Her homemade food has a scent of childhood. | | | | | |
| Father (David) | | | | | | It is ineffective in my eating. |
| Sister (Ava) | | | | She is my model in exercising. | | |

As you know, family relationships play an important role in all stages of our lives and we cannot easily restrict them because we need them. When your relationships with family members get confusing, no matter how hard you try to show yourself indifferent, you cannot hide your need for these kinds of relationships. Family relationships, especially in childhood, are fundamental and if we lose a relationship with a family member for any reason our subconscious psychological system seeks to replace it. For this reason, we become more in touch with someone who can partly satisfy our need for that particular family member. For example, if we have problems with our father, we become more intimate with our uncle. Therefore, if the relationship with family members is constructive, it can be a great help during treatment. Conversely, if this relationship is problematic, it may contribute to your failure to lose weight. Hence, finding the right strategies to reduce the impact of problematic relationships is a necessity. It's important to understand that solutions leading to abandoning your relationships with family members will not be constructive.

**Please review the table on the previous page, and if you have problematic family relationships, find strategies to manage and reduce their impact. Use the following examples to find these strategies.**

1. I want my mom to make healthier foods (like fresh and smoked salmon).
2. I have talked to my wife/husband that if s/he wants to make me happy do that by buying flowers instead of sweets.
3. With the hope that my child will have a healthier life in the future, I will explain to him/her that buying unhealthy foods should be abandoned.
4. I spend time with my friends in the park or the mountains instead of a restaurant.
5. I want my wife/husband to stop buying and keeping sugary drinks at home if my health matters to her/him.

As we said, in addition to family also our friends and colleagues affect our control of eating. Research has shown that a gluttonous friend is more likely to affect our weight than genetics. Hence reviewing the relationships with friends, colleagues at work, and peers at school is another important part of relationship engineering.

Think about your relationship with your friends and colleagues, and estimate the type of your relationship with each of them. Draw a table like the following and determine each person's state.

| Friends and colleagues | Problematic relationship | | | Constructive relationships | | | | Effectless |
|---|---|---|---|---|---|---|---|---|
| | Active | Inactive | | Active | Inactive | | | |
| | | Empowering | Provocative | | Encouraging | Modelling | Empowering | |
| Kevin | Regularly organizes gatherings and brings all the friends together in a new restaurant. | | | | | | | |
| Lexi | | | | | | | She gave me work-out clothes as a birthday present to go for a walk with her. | |
| Emma | | | She brings chips every evening. | | | | | |
| Anthony | | | | | | He has chopped fruits with himself. By looking at his colorful fruits I learn to be creative. | | |
| John | | | | | | | | My boss does not affect my eating behavior. |

Perhaps managing problematic relationships between friends and colleagues seems simpler than managing family relationships. Keep in mind you can apply your opinion about shopping or eating behavior in the family circle, but this area of discretion is limited in relationships with friends, especially colleagues. You cannot easily warn your gourmand colleague who constantly eats junk foods to limit his/her eating because of you. That's why finding the right strategies in this area is also very important.

**Think about your problematic relationships and find solutions to deal with them. Take the following examples and get ideas from them.**

1. I eat breakfast before going to work.
2. I suggest to my colleagues to give me the responsibility of breakfast preparation for one week. I begin to make changes to myself and show them new eating patterns.
3. When everyone decides to eat junk food, I will entertain myself with work and say to them that I'll join you when it's over.
4. I suggest to my friends going to the swimming pool or on a hike instead of a restaurant.

Other appropriate proceedings in the field of relationship engineering are the strengthening of effective and constructive relationships and communicating with new people or groups who can help you lose weight directly or indirectly. It is suggested for you to make new relationships with people who are living an active life and care about their health. You can go to the gym and make new friends there or if one of your friends cares about exercising, make a closer relationship with him/her and ask him/her to help and encourage you in exercising.

Brain Box
## What's going on in your brain?
Before reading this section, think about the following question:

- What is the impact of friends and relatives on creating a craving in your brain?

Remember your surroundings for a moment. What role do your mother, dad, siblings, spouse, children, friends, and even your colleagues have on your eating behavior? When do they induce cravings? As we learned in this section, different people play different roles. Imagine a mother who, whenever her overweight child goes to see her, makes french fries with fried chicken and says, "If you do not want to eat, don't! But I've made this for you." The child did not want to eat, but now he cannot resist. On the other hand, we have a mother who knows no other way to show her love rather than by cooking. It's hard to blame that mother, even though we know she's hurting her child. Imagine a party when the host says "Tonight we have no diet! You are not allowed to say I don't eat!" If you stand by what you said, your host may even be upset and think that his/her prepared meal is not good enough. An important point in the examples above is that such roles and relationships actively destroy the path of recovery because they have a strong role in your life. Now, according to what you have learned so far, can you interpret how the path is destroyed by people around you? With each exposure, there will be an outbreak in the deep areas of the brain which will have two modes:

1) Surrender to the craving, eating and deviate from the path 2) Use the energy of the control area for a break and not eating, or enter the challenge with people around you, which you will be the loser in both cases because the energy capacity is limited and will terminate soon and you will overeat again. What's your solution?

Creating constructive relationships and a gradual, calm explanation about the path you are on, creates an opportunity to begin building new relationships and discover new friends who act as role models for you.

In the end, if we look deeper into our history and culture, there were times when food was our greatest commodity, and an honor to serve to guests. Now, famine and war are in the past and we should begin new ways of showing love.

Date: ...... / ...... / ......

## Your Own Footsteps on this Journey...

**1** Provide a list of relationships that are problematic for your weight loss program and suggest strategies for managing them.

| Problematic relationships | Reformative proceedings |
|---|---|
|  |  |
|  |  |
|  |  |
|  |  |

**2** Get a complete list of relationships that play a positive role in your weight loss program and suggest strategies to improve this type of relationship.

| Constructive relationships | Confirmatory proceedings |
|---|---|
|  |  |
|  |  |
|  |  |
|  |  |

**Supplementary training:**

**① Starting an exercise** is truly a very important change in the lives of many human beings. Changing is always hard. That's why many of the people we know have never started exercising as an important activity for their health. Although changing is a difficult task, but it is quite possible if we know that for changing we should pay all "necessary fees." The fee may be worth spending the right time, paying for an exercise class, or devoting mental energy to exploring the right exercise plan for you. So, in the first step to begin physical activity, you need to be ready for spending and having a continuous investment to make this vital change in your life. Putting aside a part of your daily income and dedicating some hours of the weekly schedule for going to the nearby gyms, parks, or consulting with others in this regard can be a good start.

**② Welcome any kind of physical activity.** Performing the following activities prevents the accumulation of excess energy in the form of fat in your body:

- Climbing the office steps with the aim of burning extra calories and increasing the strength of the leg muscles.
- Park your car far away and walk to work or university.
- Carrying out groceries from nearby stores on foot.
- Having some business meetings at the park while walking.
- Having some sports equipment at home to perform physical activity when watching TV or talking on the phone.

What activities can you add to your everyday life to burn more calories?

Fat and overweight friends make you fat.
A review of personal data from more than 12,000 people has shown that the likelihood of a person becoming obese becomes 57%, 40%, and 37% if his or her friend, sibling, or spouse is obese.

| Day | Monday | Tuesday | Wednesday | Thursday | Friday | Saturday | Sunday |
|---|---|---|---|---|---|---|---|
| Weight | / / | / / | / / | / / | / / | / / | / / |

**Daily Weight Table**

## Summary:

1. You live with your memories. Rebuild your memories. You live with your loved ones by preparing healthy foods.
2. Make new interactions with your family and friends. Talk with them about changing your lifestyle. Ask them to accompany you along the way.
3. Get in new environments and find new friends for yourself. Make relationships that increase the chance of success in the new path you are taking.
4. 
5. 
6. 

---

**If you want to read more**

1. Sen, B. (2006). Frequency of family dinner and adolescent body weight status: evidence from the national longitudinal survey of youth, 1997. Obesity, 14(12), 2266-2276.

2. Christakis, N. A., & Fowler, J. H. (2007). The spread of obesity in a large social network over 32 years. New England journal of medicine, 357(4), 370-379.

Step 17     Date:   /   /

# Destructive Thoughts and Behaviors

**What behaviors or thoughts will lead me to treatment failure?**

So far, we have looked at several methods to lose weight and efforts have been made to make new changes to achieve optimal weight. Perhaps, along the way, many negative thoughts have come to your mind, and focusing on them can discourage you from continuing the treatment.

The process of change is not easy, especially holistic life changes such as those you've learned in this book so far. You should also have found any issues which can exacerbate your problems and take steps to eliminate them. You know that everything from relationships with family, friends, and colleagues to stressful life situations, both positive and negative, can affect your eating habits. It's an oversimplification to think that eating less alone will make you lose weight. It is true that ultimately, modifying all relationships and situations helps you to reduce your amount of eating. In order to do that, you needed to make serious changes to your brain processes, which we have covered in a variety of ways.

When you are trying to make changes in your life, the revelation of destructive thoughts and feelings in the treatment process is inevitable. When we get used to a pattern or system of behavior, it is difficult to change. During major life changes repeated, destructive, and harmful thoughts try to prevent this change. Therefore, it is necessary to pay attention to destructive factors that are likely to stop the recovery process. Keep in mind that cessa-

tion of recovery does not happen at once, but rather over time. So, let's look at the signs that may lead to failure of treatment. Commitment to regular study of the steps in this book, weight recording, and exercises can greatly increase your chances of success. While completing exercises to make changes, you need to be patient and note that developing skills requires much practice. Remember your childhood when you first got acquainted with the alphabet in the first year of school. At that time, you tried to learn how to read and write by yourself till you gain this skill, and now you're so innately adept at this skill you can easily read letters and words without any effort. To learn skills such as reading and writing, you must first try consciously and practice them repeatedly in different ways. After a while, you no longer need to make a conscious effort: you do it unconsciously. If you care about weight loss techniques and follow up on them, after a few months you will find that it's not hard to control your eating. Your body system manages itself without the constant need to estimate the amount of food eaten.

As discussed, one of the other important factors that can lead to a failure in the process of weight loss and recovery is to give attention to your destructive thoughts or discouragement from others. Over the course of the change, many destructive thoughts may come to your mind. Paying attention to these thoughts can make you weak on the path to weight loss, but identifying and changing them will help you to improve. You may have repeated these thoughts as internal conversations. Be careful about what you tell yourself because the excessive repetition of negative thoughts will discourage you from being treated. You can talk about these thoughts with your friends and family who support your weight loss program. Never let the destructive thoughts stay in your mind. Do not be ashamed of expressing them. Keep in mind that not every thought that comes to our mind is logical. We must learn to evaluate our thoughts and, according to the correct principles, identify our intellectual errors.

**Destructive thoughts can be divided into four major categories:**
1. Thoughts that attack the target. For example, one assumes that choosing to lose weight as a goal will conflict with proper maternal behavior or being a good spouse.
2. Thoughts that question the path. Thoughts like, "the path is too long and time-consuming and costly."

3. *Thoughts that question the means of achieving the goal. Like, whether obesity has a genetic cause or not, "is it possible to lose weight by participating in group therapy and talking about yourself?"*
4. *Thoughts that question the healing process. For example, You've got so much weight loss and you're tired, now it's okay if you want to take a few days off.*

**The following are examples of destructive thoughts, please read them carefully:**

- This program takes too long, I'm not in the mood for it and I want to lose weight very quickly.
- I do not have enough time to study regularly, follow this book step by step, and complete all of the exercises.
- Evaluating myself to understand what conditions are associated with overeating is very time-consuming.
- I do not need to do these exercises. I know myself perfectly.
- I cannot change my environment because it's not under my control.
- I prefer to be a good mother or wife and cook delicious food, rather than inconvenience others by losing weight.
- Gluttonous friends and colleagues do not affect me and I do not have to limit my relationship with them.
- Everyone likes chubby people more.
- My husband gets so angry when I don't eat dinner with him. Maintaining marital life is more important than losing weight.
- Everyone in our family has obesity, and so far, no one has succeeded in overcoming it.
- If losing weight is so hard, I prefer to remain obese.
- Who said that losing weight makes you feel good? I know a lot of healthy fat people!
- In this world, there are more important things than weight loss.
- Some people are genetically obese and you cannot do anything for them.
- My parents are the main reason for my obesity by overfeeding me in my childhood, and now I cannot do anything.
- Has anyone ever been able to lose weight and keep it off?
- If someone loves me, then s/he should accept me for who I am.

All these thoughts are made by your "chubby mind," which wants to resist weight loss and keep you away from losing weight and being healthy.

Paying attention to destructive errors and thoughts is very important. Some of them can be very deceptive, and if you do not pay attention, you can fail over and over again. For example, "Now that I am modifying my behavior and I'm losing weight for a while, it is better to leave it for a few days and eat as much as I want!" You need to be careful about modifying your thoughts and behaviors. Like health, this is a life long process. Interrupting or rolling back on destructive thoughts causes irreparable damage to your recovery path. It should be noted that this type of justification, is due to the parts of the brain associated with food. These kinds of false thoughts must be confronted.

In addition to thoughts, our behaviors can also hurt our recovery. Destructive behaviors may not even be directly related to eating behaviors but can still have an impact on your weight loss journey.

**Here are some of these behaviors:**

- Not considering enough time to study and review the steps of the book.
- Sleeping deprivation during the period of weight loss.
- Working too hard and getting tired during treatment.
- Elimination of recreational activities.
- Spending the money that was saved for non-eating recreational activities.
- Resisting to buy a scale for weighing.
- Joking and mocking book tutorials.
- Minimizing your mistakes and not reporting them during exercises.
- Justifying yourself when not doing book exercises or blaming others.
- Planning dinner and lunch parties at a time when you're losing weight.
- Lack of financial investment and time to find and start a proper exercise routine.

Paying attention to destructive behaviors is very important. We must think about them thoroughly and be aware of them. Awareness is the first and most important step in coping with these thoughts and behaviors.

### Brain Box
# What's going on in your brain?
Before reading this section, think about the following question:

- How will your brain processes prevent weight loss?

People who are overweight often find interesting ways to minimize their weight problems. For example, they say, "Because people around me eat a lot, I'm obese", "We're genetically obese", " I'm obese because of the stress of my job", "I haven't cared until now, I will lose weight when it matters." All of these statements have one thing in common: People often find obesity to be very simple and think they can lose weight whenever they want. Those who have experienced it know losing weight is not an easy task. You are now familiar with its complexities. To try this out, do the following experiment: Tell people there are two ways to lose weight, 1) Eat less and lose weight 2) Increase their brain's ability to manage eating. They will usually choose the first one because it is based on the fact that they are not part of the problem. When we say change yourself and accept that something is wrong, that acceptance can be painful. People come up with justifications to relieve themselves of this stress. For example, imagine a forty-year-old doctor who performs difficult daily surgeries, teaching students and hospital management at the same time, along with all of this, failing to manage his weight. Now eating is a bitter experience which he faces every day. By trying to justify and attribute the causes of this problem to factors other than himself, he strives to find peace and balance, and if he does not, life becomes a hell that is hard to bear. But where is the brain in our story?

The brain functions based on its evolutionary experience and it loves stability. It also considers any changes as danger and does its best to bring the situation back to its original state. For example, a person whose weight was 250 lbs most of his life reaches 175 lbs; the brain considers this change a threat and tries to make up the lost weight by reducing metabolism. He cannot burn the same number of calories as other 175 lb men, meaning, he has to consume 500 to 400 calories less a day to maintain his weight.

Dependency on bad eating behavior activates the brain's reward and pleasure circuits, and the brain is always looking to regain that pleasure. The next time you have a debilitating thought, know that your stubborn and dependent brain is looking for pleasure, so ignore it and try to follow the instructions of this book. Remember, your dependent brain needs time to regulate. By reading through the teachings of this book, give your brain the tools and time to rearrange. The excellent performance of your non-dependent brain to manage your eating behavior without any pressure will make you excited.

Date: ...... / ...... / ......

## Your Own Footsteps on this Journey...

**1** Again, read the list of destructive thoughts and misleading justifications. Think about the thoughts that can interfere with your recovery process and how you can modify them.

| Destructive thought | Alternative thought |
|---|---|
| I know a lot of obese people. | Seeing a few healthy obese individuals does not change the facts. Scientific studies show that the possibility of illness and death in obese people is several times higher than healthy-weight people. |

**2** What behaviors can provide the basis of failure in your recovery path? Provide a list of these destructive behaviors that directly and indirectly lead you to overeat and being overweight. Awareness of these behaviors is an important step in starting their management.

① 

② 

③ 

④ 

⑤ 

⑥ 

Consider water as your main drink, because water increases metabolism and reduces appetite. Order mineral water in the restaurants instead of soft drinks and try to have a bottle of water next to you at work and home.

Some people think that ab workouts will lead to a skinnier midsection. This is a false belief! Your body fat is distributed and burned throughout your body, during consciously eating and physical activity. To burn the fats in one area of the body, you can not only exercise in the targeted area. Exercising that strengthens the abdominal muscles can give a better shape to your abdomen by tightening the abdominal wall but does not affect the local fat loss.

If you want to burn your abdominal fat, you need to reduce the amount of energy intake to the entire body and increase the energy consumption of the whole body.

| Day | Monday / / | Tuesday / / | Wednesday / / | Thursday / / | Friday / / | Saturday / / | Sunday / / |
|---|---|---|---|---|---|---|---|
| Weight | | | | | | | |

Daily Weight Table

## Summary:

1. Program failure and relapse to the previous condition does not happen all at once.
2. Disruptive thoughts and behaviors are the cause of relapse. Therefore, they should be considered a danger and taken seriously.
3. Identifying, classifying, and being aware of destructive thoughts and behaviors will help to manage and reduce their incidence.
4. Your dependent brain is always waiting for the best time to deviate from the path you have chosen.
5. 
6.

Step 18    Date: ... / ... / ...

# Amplifying Inhibitory Control

**How to improve your brain's ability to inhibit craving?**

The human brain is the center of our sensory, behavioral, emotional, and cognitive experience. The brain observes the surrounding environment, affects it and binds past and present. The brain is divided into several parts. We want to introduce you to two parts, which are related to eating behaviors. The first part, which is located in lower and deep areas, is called Limbic, and its task is to create desire and craving for food. Reward areas are also located in this area, and the activity of it makes you feel pleasure. The activity of this area is also associated with our emotions, especially sorrow, fear, anger, and hatred. When we behave rashly and without control based on our tendencies, feelings, or emotions, we are under the control of this area of the brain. The next area we want to introduce is the frontal cortex; this area is associated with thinking, attention, judgment, social behaviors, and the sequential implementation of targeted actions. If this area is damaged, your ability to think and judge and the power of your social behaviors will be reduced. Also, this region can restrain the limbic center and prevent experiencing immediate and contemporary enjoyment. Therefore, stimulating and empowering this area can help control cravings or overeating behaviors.

One of the important things to know about the frontal cortex is that the activities of this area require a lot of energy and we cannot use this region for a long time. Perhaps you've experienced many times at the beginning of the day that you are able to make decisive, challenging, and complicated decisions, but you are left feeling tired afterwards. In these circumstances, you may be having trouble managing your overeating at lunch or dinner time. So, given the limited power of this area, we need to know when and where to use this energy. Learning new knowledge and skills requires using this area, and if we waste its energy on unnecessary things we won't be able to accomplish our goals. You may have noticed that during emotionally stressful situations, regulating your emotions can leave you feeling tired emotionally in stressful situations and then you have to inhibit your emotions by using the brain's frontal cortex, which you will feel very tired and running out of energy. In this state, it is very difficult to control the craving for eating.

**Self-deprivation management strategies can be divided into three main categories:**

- Ways of reducing consumption "Self-Active"
- Ways of filling your treasury "Self-Active"
- Ways of increasing the capacity of your treasury "Self-Active"

In the following, we will first discuss the situations that lead to depletion and then provide solutions to fill and increase the capacity of your treasury.

**Read the following examples.**

① Early in the morning, my boss rejected a project I had struggled with for a month. He described the work as elementary and crude. When I left the room, I couldn't walk. I felt very tired and numb. I went back to my office and ate everything I had.

② I argued with my wife. She didn't like the dress I had bought for her birthday. She didn't appreciate my efforts to make her happy. I was sick as a parrot. I left the house, went to the closest restaurant, and ate as much as I could.

Keep in mind that the efficient use of energy in the frontal cortex can help you inhibit craving and relief by other strategies for weight loss management. Therefore, it's best to take some distance from activities that reduce the energy of the frontal cortex.

These activities include:

① Inappropriate discussions and emotional conflicts are two of the important factors in reducing the energy of the frontal cortex. So, at least in the first few months of your weight loss program, seriously avoid wasting energy on emotional challenges like family discussions, disagreement with friends or colleagues, and unnecessary anger. The feeling of rejection in emotional relationships is a serious factor in the evacuation of energy in the areas of the frontal cortex.

② Repeated and unnecessary decisions reduce the energy of the frontal cortex. Unnecessary decisions at work that can be made by others too, such as "percentage of salary increase," or "what rewards to consider," or "buying chair A or chair B," can lead to an inappropriate reduction of energy in the frontal cortex. Waking up at a specific time, having a prepared breakfast, and exercising on a consistent schedule all reduce the energy consumption of the frontal cortex. This saved energy can now be used to inhibit cravings.

**Consider the following examples of activities which waste the energy in the frontal cortex:**

① Inappropriate discussions with family and friends.
② Listening to the sad news about the situation in the country.
③ Deciding on the right dress and shoes.
④ Trying to argue with someone who does not accept everything logically.
⑤ Sleep deprivation.
⑥ Undertaking various responsibilities.

Paying attention to happiness and increased self-satisfaction is one of the things that can help you to strengthen the activities of the frontal cortex. For example, caring about and encouraging yourself, paying attention to progress, expressing gratitude for those who are happy with your progress and encourage you, paying attention to your appearance and your beauty, wearing well-fitting clothes, watching your body in the mirror, doing your makeup, etc. All of these can help you fill the energy of the frontal cortex. Learn how to care about yourself and keep in mind that the main purpose of this program is to learn how to use your brain properly.

Another way you can make more use of your brain's frontal cortex is to increase the amount of energy stored in the area. This is difficult and takes a lot of time but it is feasible. How can this source become bigger? Doing the exercises below can help you strengthen your frontal cortex. Activities like:

- Writing with your non-dominant hand.
- Performing activities that require concentration, such as yoga and meditation, archery or throwing darts, and stretching exercises.
- The correct form of sitting and standing, especially when you are studying, will have a good effect on your focus. The body when sitting should be like an exclamation point, straight, and not curved like a question mark.
- Doing activities that increase the level of attention and concentration, such as solving crosswords, Sudoku, computer games, intellectual games, puzzles, and Rubik's cubes.
- Doing religious practices or meditation with deep attention.
- Listening to calming music while watching your breathing movements.
- Writing memories and daily tasks regularly.
- Visualizing landscapes, sounds, smells, tastes, and other senses, like imagining a garden and making a picture of it with all the details you expect to see or hear in a garden, like trees and flowers with different sizes and colors, sounds you hear such as birds singing, insects chirping, and the rustling of leaves, or the sound of the wind, even the feeling of heat or cold.
- Solving math exercises and intelligence tests daily.
- Learning a new language for regular weekly sessions.
- Companionship with brainy people.
- Seeing and touching the beauty of nature regularly, even daily.
- Detailed and daily recording of economic activities such as costs and revenues.

But in addition to strengthening the brain's frontal cortex, you can also control your limbic activity. Preventing the activation of these areas by avoiding the occurrence of triggers is one of the ways to control the limbic region because triggers can activate the deep limbic areas, and the high activity of this region leads to immediate behaviors that will be difficult to control. Hence, as much as you think about preventing strategies of triggers and use them, the activity of these areas decreases and there is no need to use frontal cortex to inhibit limbic areas. Under these circumstances, your ability to control overeating will increase.

**Brain Box**

# What's going on in your brain?

Before reading this section, think about the following question:

- Have you ever heard of the cognitive triangle in the frontal?

In previous sessions, we discussed the deep (limbic) and frontal areas of the brain and their role in the control and their limited capacity. In this step, we try to take a closer look at the frontal area. So far, we have found that the upper part of the frontal has a control area that inhibits the deep areas which have a pleasure outburst and the propensity to eat. Besides this inhibitory area, there is a segment between the two hemispheres in the frontal of the brain called saliency that gives the power of interpretation and analysis. Because one's eating management is based on the interpretation of eating signals and we said that if one becomes successful in reappraisal, the "managed and initiated" craving will no longer have the previous power. Next to these areas, there is another section in the lower part of the frontal called the verbalization areas. The person uses these areas to consciously talk about the phenomenon of eating and to manage it based on the knowledge created; So, there is a cognitive triangle in the frontal that gives the person the ability to manage the deep areas of the brain.

In addition to these areas, there are other sections in the frontal area that we will address them in the next sessions. Here's an example to clarify: Suppose you go to a party and see a variety of stimulating foods at the self-service reception table; the deep areas begin their outburst, but you are going to analyze every single food in your mind, like what are the ingredients? How much oil is used? What is its benefit? Is it homemade or mass-produced? How much should I eat? Will I feel better or I would regret it? should I

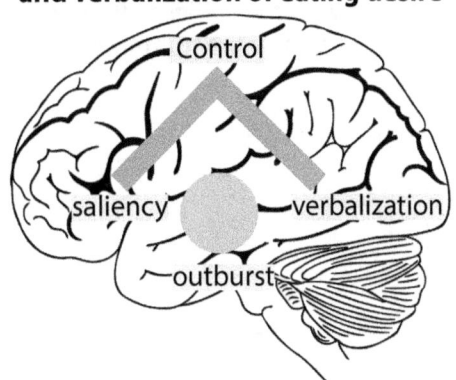

**the brain's circuits of self-awareness and verbalization of eating desire**

share the food? Should I eat by the table or go indoors? should I take a small plate or a big one?

**After you do the initial analysis,**

- Use the smallest plate.
- Try only one type of food because tasting different foods will increase cravings.
- Eat only once and take a good look at the amount that is going to get into your body before eating.
- Use a fork as much as possible with the non-dominant hand because it slows down the speed of eating.
- Have an inner discussion from the beginning when you see the triggers until the meal is over.
- In the end, try to talk about the experience you had with other members of the therapeutic group or family and tell of your potential.
- Each of the above strategies involves one or more of the three regions of the frontal cortex with inhibition, reappraisal, and verbalization.

Date: ...... / ...... / ......

## Your Own Footsteps on this Journey...

**1** What activities or situations do you have in your daily life that causes energy loss in the area of the frontal cortex? Make a list of these situations or activities and score the amount of energy reduction through these activities from zero to ten.

| Situations or activities that reduce the energy of the frontal cortex | Scoring from 0 to 10 |
|---|---|
|  |  |

**2** What things or events during the day make you feel that the energy of your frontal cortex has increased to manage the craving? Rate the impact of these things or events from zero to ten.

| Situations or activities that increase the energy of the frontal cortex | Scoring from (0 ta 10) |
| --- | --- |
|  |  |
|  |  |
|  |  |
|  |  |

**3** Under what conditions, the deep limbic areas in your brain are activated so much that the energy of the frontal cortex is not enough to inhibit them? Make a list of these conditions.

**4** Read the list of activities that increase the amount of energy in the frontal cortex. Of these, select 5 activities that you can do or you are interested in them and set up a contract to do one of them.

1. 
2. 
3. 
4. 
5. 

> Small contract for changing:
>
> I _____ Commit myself, based on the commitment and duty that I am given to my weight loss; this week
>
> Agreement date:            Your signature:

## Health note 18:

"Walk more."

You can park your car farther and walk more. You also know that it is better to use stairs instead of the elevator.

| Day | Monday | Tuesday | Wednesday | Thursday | Friday | Saturday | Sunday |
|---|---|---|---|---|---|---|---|
| | / / | / / | / / | / / | / / | / / | / / |
| Weight | | | | | | | |

**Daily Weight Table**

## Summary:

1. The parts responsible for controlling the brain play an important role in eating behavior.
2. The brain's energy is limited for self-control, and this limited energy must be used correctly and tactfully.
3. Strategies for managing this energy are divided into three categories: 1. Consumption reduction 2. Filling the treasury 3. Increasing capacity of the treasury.
4. Learning the brain's energy management skills helps a lot in the process of self-control and ultimately in managing eating behavior.
5. 
6. 

---

If you want to read more

1. Stuss, D. T., & Knight, R. T. (Eds.). (2013). Principles of frontal lobe function. Oxford University Press.
2. Salloway, S. P., Malloy, P. F., & Duffy, J. D. (Eds.). (2008). The frontal lobes and neuropsychiatric illness. American Psychiatric Pub.
3. Wolpert, S. (2007). Putting Feelings Into Words Produces Therapeutic Effects in the Brain; UCLA Neuroimaging Study Supports Ancient Buddhist Teachings. UCLA Newsroom, June, 21, 132-38.

Step 19   Date: ..... / ..... / .....

# Habitual Eating and Eating Habits

**How do you identify and modify bad eating habits?**

The examination of various factors leading to overeating has been mentioned for many reasons so far, and you've learned a lot about the causes of obesity and being overweight. In this step, we try to get you acquainted with one of the other causes of obesity which is the wrong behavioral habits. With a little contemplation of your behavior and the behavior of those who are overweight, you will notice that more or less all of these people have inappropriate eating habits. Habitual behaviors are done rapidly and with minimal awareness, so they do not consume a lot of energy. Many people are not aware of these habits, and they are hard to change. So another step that you have to take to achieve your goals in this program is to identify wrong eating habits. To learn more about this, let's first define the habit and give examples for it. A habit is a learned behavior that has been repeated frequently and has become a part of our behavioral characteristics. If we do not do it we feel uncomfortable and think that we've lost something or something is not perfect in life. Such as, "I'm used to having french fries for lunch and if I do not eat it, my lunch wouldn't be complete", "I'm used to eating bread with every meal", "I'm used to having a sweet after eating my meal.", or "I'm used to drinking tea with sugar." These examples of eating are not triggered by cravings, nor in

response to hunger, but because you have been doing it for a long time, and have become accustomed to this type of eating. You may not even remember much of your eating habits right now.

Some of these habits have a cultural aspect, such as having french fries and heavy meals at a party or eating during holidays and celebrations, otherwise, it is not pleasurable or perfect. There is a difference between "habits" and "craving," although both conditions can lead to overeating. In eating induced by craving, you eat after a confrontation with a trigger, you get hot thoughts and then crave, and you eat because you cannot control this craving. Like when you have a depressed mood and constantly eat junk foods during the day until the negative mood is reduced. But when people have a bad habit, they do that habit without triggers. For example, many of us bring sugar, soft drinks, rice, french fries, or bread to the table without any cravings. If a person does not behave according to their habit, it does not feel good. As a result, he feels anxious and imagines that something is not working properly!

There are a number of bad eating habits that lead to overeating, such as eating standing up, eating fast, not drinking plenty of water throughout the day, drinking too much tea or coffee, having large portions and unhealthy food, eating hot food and rushing, eating lots of salty foods, drinking soft drinks, eating fatty foods, eating at night, and many other bad habits.

Please take a look at the list of eating habits expressed by different people. Think about yourself and see which of these behaviors you are doing inappropriately.

### Wrong behavioral habits as an underlying factor of overeating

After eating a meal, I have to eat something sweet.

If there is no bread at the table, no one will feel full.

I am not used to drinking water.

I have to drink a cola while eating my meal.

Foods like beans and lentils should be eaten with bread.

I am used to eating something before bedtime. I sleep better with my belly full.

During the day I drink several cups of tea without realizing it.

Now that your behavioral habits have been identified, you need a plan to change them. As mentioned earlier, changing habits is not easy to do, because in many cases we are not aware of what we are doing. Eliminating any behavioral habit may not be easy to accomplish and requires significant amounts of energy and time. You may experience an unpleasant feeling by leaving your habits which you have to deal with them for a while. Perhaps you have repeatedly heard that "old habits die hard." This is true because when you leave a habit, you will have bad feelings for a while until you get used to the new condition over time. Therefore, this path should be done step-by-step, and, perhaps, with the supervision of your therapist. For example, one of the bad eating habits is "glutting" because you're used only stopping when your stomach is completely full. To eliminate this habit, you must first have a specific diet plan for yourself. Specify your food intake before eating and do not put more than that on your plate. After you have eaten your food, if it is less than your usual food and you are still hungry, do not worry, the satiety message is received by the brain 20 minutes after the first bite, give your brain time. Other things you can do to get rid of your bad habits while eating is to look at the food closely before eating. Smell it, chew slowly, and touch the food with your tongue and teeth. Slowly taste your food and activate your sense of taste. Listen to your chewing sound. In this case, you have used all your five senses for eating, which makes the food more delicious. Your rate of eating becomes very slow and you get full earlier.

Drink plenty of water throughout the day. Try to always have a small bottle of water with you. Keep bottles of mineral water in your car or at your office, so you always have it with you. Decrease the habit of drinking tea, coffee, or soft drinks, even consuming dietary drinks can increase your appetite, ultimately causing you to become overweight. The habit of eating a variety of spices, sauce, or pickles also increases appetite, leading to obesity.

**So in conclusion, the following steps can be taken to modify eating habits:**

① Identifying your bad eating habits: **Finding bad eating habits and preparing a list of them is one of the most important steps to correct them. Many of these habits are hidden in our everyday lives, and finding and indexing them requires time and energy.

② Determine the difficulty of not doing the habit and severity of an unpleasant feeling caused by any of the habits: **Not doing the habits is somewhat difficult, and can create unpleasant feelings. Determine the severity of your bad habits concerning these two features. For example, if you decide to eat lunch at a restaurant, do not order bread or french fries with chicken, and instead choose chicken with salad. Making this decision is very hard at the moment when the waitress is standing next to you. How bad is your feeling after making this decision, and after leaving the restaurant? By determining your level of anxiety, you can determine your dependency on each bad eating habits.

❸ Selecting habits one by one and replacing them at the right time: Changing or leaving eating habits requires energy and time, and it's not possible to do it all at once. Start with the hardest habits that have the most impact on you, like drinking soft drinks with every meal. Change habits step by step. For example, replace the soft drinks with water, at one meal per day, and eventually, at every meal. When you are tired or too busy, it's not good to choose new habits and correct bad habits. It's best to choose one of your bad habits at the right time, encounter the uncomfortable feelings for a few days, and eventually leave them behind.

❹ Creating new and valuable habits in recovery path: Along with bad eating habits, good habits can exist or come into existence, such as the habit of taking a morning walk, the habit of consuming fruit throughout the day, the habit of using whole-grain bread instead of bread full of starches, not eating between meals, eating a salad before meals, walking in the park with friends and family. Creating the right habits is also difficult, like breaking previous bad habits, and can be time-consuming. The trick to creating new behaviors is repeating them at certain times and making sure you enjoy each effort. If you take walks in a place you enjoy, and at a regular convenient time, the habit will form. If you don't enjoy walking before work, then it will become very difficult to solidify this habit.

**To create new habits, you need to keep in mind a few important points:**

❶ Use reminders at first. For a behavior to become a habit, it must be accompanied by a signal. It is best to relate it to specific times during the day. For example, in the morning before going to work or after your spouse and children leave for the day.

❷ Being enjoyable. For a behavior to become a habit, at the very least, must be fun.

For example, if you want to make exercise a habit for yourself, you should choose a sport that is enjoyable for you.

❸ Constant and repetitive. To turn a behavior into a habit, you need to do it repeatedly and in a consistent manner. Constant steps, constant form, and constant repetitive process form a habit.

So, in short, it can be said: "Consistent behaviors will become habits if you can do them with enjoyment at specific times of the day.

Brain Box
# What's going on in your brain?
Before reading this section, think about the following question:

- How does habitual eating control the brain?

So far, whenever we talked about eating, one of its dimensions has been craving and triggers; in this step, a new dimension is added to the causes of overeating that is known as habitual eating. How are habits created or diminished? To better understand this, we will use a real-life example.

Has it ever happened to you that you have not brushed your teeth for a while? How did you feel?

Many people in modern societies have become accustomed to brushing so that if they do not brush one day, they will feel bad. But has that been the case from the beginning?

In the 1920s -1930s, the situation was not the same, and one of the three major problems of the US military was the military's oral health. Most of them had tooth decay and only ten percent of them brushed their teeth. To address this, the US Department of Health provided training on the benefits of brushing, and after ten years, only about five to six percent added to the number of people brushing.

There was no toothpaste at that time, and people cleaned their teeth with special powders. Concurrent with this health challenge, some companies began to produce new products related to oral hygiene. The first company to come up with the concept of toothpaste was "Pepsodent." The company worked for ten years but had little success and was on the verge of bankruptcy because people did not brush and, consequently, toothpaste was not sold. They were looking for a marketer for advertising, and someone called Claude C. Hopkins accepted this challenge. He had to get people used to brushing. Over twenty years, he managed to convince over fifty percent of the Amer-

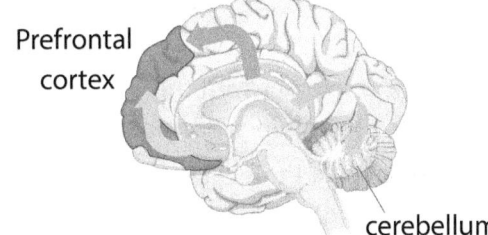

ican population to brush. But how did he manage to encourage this new habit? In order to develop a new habit, we first need a trick to remember to do it. The first sign that came to Hopkins' mind was tooth whiteness so that whenever a person stands in front of a mirror and sees his yellow teeth, he will be encouraged to brush. That was not a helpful sign, because people rarely saw their teeth in the mirror during the day. Hopkins had to look for another sign to use. Hence, tooth plaque came to his mind! When you touch your teeth with tongue, you can feel the plaque, although it is not always negative and is part of the normal physiology of the mouth. Hopkins used it as a sign because it is very common during the day for people to touch their teeth and feel the plaque. This would make the person feel a bit dirtier and brush more. It had not yet become a habit since one component was missing- pleasure. So, he began to look for a way to add pleasure to the toothbrushing experience. Meanwhile, he found peppermint oil, which was crisp and cool. He combined it with toothpaste to use as a reward for the brain. Because of the coolness, people thought their mouths were clean and enjoyed brushing more, while the mint had nothing to do with cleanliness. In this way, he was able to form a positive habit in society. Once you have become familiar with a successful example that cleverly uses the three components of a habit-formation; now it is your turn to come up with habits that are incidentally related to eating.

When people start overeating because of the triggers or when they crave, the deep and frontal areas of the brain are activated. The deep areas are activated and the pleasurable outburst begins and based on the reaction of the forntal areas brekes, eating or not eating will hoppen. Suppose you are sitting in a room but you have ice-cream in the fridge and you are fighting over whether to eat it or not. If someone asked you to do something else, you might forget the ice-cream and focus on the work you have to do. For some people eating is an obligation. They think, "Food is not attractive to me and I don't have many cravings for it, but I have to eat. I have to eat a lot, otherwise I won't feel good. Even if there is something I need to do, I will postpone it so I can eat." In this case, the dorsal part of the brain begins to act and interact with the cerebellum. When the cerebellum is activated, it helps to get things done automatically without anyone noticing them.

We have had this cycle in many of our experiences. When we enjoy doing something, the frontal areas of the brain become activated and when that task becomes habitual, the dorsal areas of the brain begin to function. So, it makes sense to choose a habit that comes with pleasure first. Otherwise, it will never become a habit.

Date: ...... / ...... / ......

## Your Own Footsteps on this Journey...

**1** **Please write down your behavioral bad habits in the table below and suggest solutions to modify them:**

| Behavioral bad habits | Solutions to modify them |
|---|---|
| I used to have a piece of sweet after eating lunch to change the taste of my mouth. | I can brush my teeth instead of eating sweets. |
| I used to eat bread with all my meals. | I can satiate myself without eating bread by practicing. |

**2** **What are the right habits that do not exist in you and how can be created?**

| Right habits | How can I create them |
|---|---|
|  |  |

**3** **Settle a contract to eliminate any bad eating habits and creating the new right habits.**

Small contract for changing:

I ........... Commit myself, based on the commitment and duty that I am given to my weight loss; this week

Agreement date:                    Your signature:

## Health note 19:

Smell Banana, Apple, or Mint. A study conducted on more than 3,000 people in Chicago showed that people, who smell foods, feel full sooner. Researchers believe that smelling while eating will stimulate your brain in a way that you will feel full sooner.

| Day | Monday | Tuesday | Wednesday | Thursday | Friday | Saturday | Sunday |
|---|---|---|---|---|---|---|---|
|  | / / | / / | / / | / / | / / | / / | / / |
| Weight |  |  |  |  |  |  |  |

**Daily Weight Table**

## Summary:

1. Part of your overeating is due to behavioral habits, not the need or desire to eat.
2. To deal with habits, we must first know them and find out about them.
3. Severe behavioral habits become compulsive, which means that getting rid of them will be very difficult.
4. Encounter the negative emotions of quitting and accept them as a natural part of quitting and know that they are transient.
5. Overcome negative habits by creating new habits.
6. To form a habit, be careful with reminders, repetitive constant behaviors, rewarding, and enjoyable components.
7. 
8. 

If you want to read more

1. Smith KS, Graybiel AM. Habit formation. Dialogues Clin Neurosci. 2016;18(1):33-43.

**Step 20**  Date: .... / .... / ....

# Supporting Activities for Recovery

**What actions or thoughts lead me forward in the path of health?**

In the previous steps, you became familiar with some of the thoughts and destructive behaviors in the weight loss journey. In this step, you will get acquainted with the practices and activities that will help you in the recovery process. In order to stay on this path, you need to learn how to take care of your recovery process. Some thoughts and behaviors can be destructive to your recovery journey, while others are helpful to your treatment and recovery.

✎ **Consider these examples.**

### Helpful thoughts

Finally, I was able to resolve the problem that bothered me for years.

This treatment is based on science and helps me understand myself.

If others can lose weight, so can I.

By changing myself, I can make beneficial changes in my family.

Now that I care about my health, I can be a better mother.

By now you have changed your overeating behaviors by studying the book, but you must remember that changing the mindset and behaviors is not an easy task. Perhaps, over the course of your recovery, you have had doubts about the possibility of weight loss. However, what's important is that you have continued to study this book until this step. This is a great success and you will certainly see its results soon. As previously mentioned, our destructive and negative thoughts can keep us from the continuation of treatment; on the other hand, our positive and constructive thoughts make us more hopeful in continuing treatment. Below, we refer to thoughts and beliefs that will strengthen you to stay in the treatment.

**Please repeat the following supporting thoughts to yourself.**

- I must do all the necessary things to lose weight until I achieve success.
- I must plan my life such that it supports my sports, activities, and weight loss program because I deserve to be the top priority.
- A desire to eat does not necessarily mean that I am hungry or that I have to eat.
- I'm not concerned about satiety; I know it takes 20 minutes to feel full.
- It makes no difference whether I pour excess food in the trash or in my stomach! In either case, it is a waste. To eat more than what the body needs is an even bigger waste because it threatens my health.
- I eat slowly and in a seated position; I think about what I eat so that I can enjoy it.
- I should not expect my weight loss to happen quickly. For this treatment to work, I must be patient.
- If I am feeling bad, eating does not help me to solve the problem. It's better to think of a solution that doesn't involve eating.
- Accepting my current weight, determining an "appropriate weight", and doing physical activity are important values in my life and my commitment to change over time in order to achieve these values should be the most important priority of my life in the coming years.
- Losing weight makes me feel better about myself.
- My kids need a healthy mother, not a fat and sick mother.
- Losing weight improves my relationship with my partner.
- My colleagues treat me more respectfully since I have lost weight.

Be mindful of the positive and supportive thoughts in your recovery path. Repeat them to yourself out loud, over and over again, or write them in the form of sentences on a small paper and carry them with you. Wherever you feel that you cannot perform the tasks, read the related content again. Make sure you remember the book tutorials and exercises; you can even give them to your family members. As you know, if thoughts are repeated in our minds frequently, they become an attitude, and the right attitude leads to proper behavior. When thoughts change, it's easier to change the behavior, but changing behavior without changing thoughts and attitudes is not easy.

Also, along with changing thoughts and choosing helpful ones instead of destructive ones, executing the right actions will help our treatment. Actions like:

1. **Regular weighing during recovery.**
2. **Doing exercises at specific times.**
3. **Commitment to the contracts set during the study of this book.**
4. **Demystifying your ambiguities with the help of professionals in the field of eating behavior.**
5. **Participating in the treatment sessions and expressing your feelings and thoughts during the sessions.**
6. **Being mindful of the importance of happiness and finding appropriate ways to increase the quality of a happy and healthy life.**
7. **Being mindful of the importance of having fun and planning the right time for fun activities.**
8. **Maintaining your motivation while studying this book and implementing its recommendations.**
9. **Gaining support from people who can help you along your recovery path.**
10. **Managing your relationship with people who might hurt your treatment.**
11. **Being assertive and guard your boundaries; "saying NO" to the offers and insistence of others to eat.**
12. **Paying attention to the change of bad habitual behaviors regarding eating.**
13. **Being mindful of the importance of cognitive development and expressing it to family members and others.**
14. **Reviewing the recovery process and analysis of the level of your modified thoughts and behaviors, from the beginning step of the book up to now.**

15. **Commitment to a daily exercise program and doing it regularly.**
16. **Buying low-calorie fruits and vegetables such as cucumbers, carrots, lettuce, etc. regularly and preparing healthy meals, such as grilled chicken, ahead of time.**
17. **Keeping a bottle of mineral water at home or work.**
18. **Contacting friends who can help you feel better in the case of severe cravings.**

During the previous steps of this book, we have provided you with a wide range of appropriate suggestions for designing supportive weight loss programs. However, just knowing about these methods is not enough for implementing them and achieving the goal of weight loss.

**You will need to follow the steps below to implement the suggested list:**

1. Provide a well-defined outline, detailing the implementation of effective weight loss activities that work for you.

2. Commitment to achieving the value of weight loss with earnestness, patience, and stability. Spending considerable time and carrying the financial costs required in the provided list represents your executive commitment.

3. Select the listed options one by one, sign a small personal contract for each option. Do them at a specific time, and mark the options that are done on your list.

4. Evaluate how each activity is performed and examine the obstacles and challenges that arise as a result of its implementation, then change or modify if necessary. You can also choose another activity that is more practical, useful and effective for you.

Performing these steps will ensure you move towards weight loss and maintain it over time.

Brain Box

## What's going on in your brain?

Before reading this section, think about the following questions:

- What exercises can boost brain networks to manage cravings?
- What types of brain activity can be categorized as supportive behaviors?

In previous sessions of the book, you were introduced to two types of important brain networks: the Default Mode Network (DMN) and the Executive Control Network (ECN), and you learned under what conditions they were activated and how they needed another network called the Saliency Network to switch between them.

**If we compare these networks to the gears of a car, how would their similarity be explained?**

We all know that a car's gears make it possible to perform different functions under different conditions. For example, when starting the car at high-speed, uphill/downhill, or reverse gear the car will work differently based on the gear used.

But can our brains also work in different gears? That is, when it is in gear "A" it has some abilities rather than when it is in gear "B". The brain acts very emotionally in gear "A" and very reasonably in gear "B". Think about this question for a while and review your personal experiences. Do you have a similar experience with your brain?

Often, we don't know much about how our brain functions. If we consider our brain as a gearbox, it is an "automatic" one and the gears shift in such a way that we are not aware of them. When a person is in certain situations like starvation, some of his/her brain processes, like those that are related to reasoning or inhibiting behavior, do not work properly but other parts of the brain keep their function. For some people, work and family pressures have overwhelmed the Executive Control Network, so that the Default Mode Network is outdated and out of its normal functioning. One of the exercises for switching the Executive Control Network to the Default Mode Network is coloring. It should be emphasized that studies show that there are different activities that can help you boost your Default Mode Network. For example, while facing an emotional conflict or problems, reading highly engaging stories or practicing yoga and meditation can be useful in activating the Default Mode Network at least for a short period. There is, perhaps, nothing as available and doable as a few minutes of coloring to activate the Default Mode Network. The effectiveness of these exercises, like any other exercise, varies from person to person, and our experience shows that the greater you improve your skills in applying these exercises, the more you will understand the depth of their effects. On the other hand, studies show that people who spend time immersing themselves in the Default Mode Network and then coming out again, which means drowning in themselves and then activating the Executive Control Network; the person achieves the ability to manage his/her eating behavior or any other desire. The experience of shifting between these two networks in the brain is an important supporting behavior and helps improve the quality and speed of the treatment process. Here are some exercises to familiarize you with how to strengthen your Default Mode Network.

Date: ...... / ...... / ......

## Your Own Footsteps on this Journey...

**1** Please provide a list of supporting activities for yourself. Score the effectiveness of each of these activities on the onset and continuation of the recovery path from zero to one hundred.

| Supporting activities | Effectiveness |
|---|---|
|  |  |

**2** **Please select one of the supportive activities and set up a contract for its implementation:**

> Small contract for changing:
>
> I ........... Commit myself, based on the commitment and duty that I am given to my weight loss; this week
>
> 
>
> Agreement date: .................... Your signature: ....................

**3** **Please provide a list of supporting thoughts for yourself. Score the effectiveness of each of these thoughts on the onset and continuation of the recovery path from 0-100.**

| Supporting thoughts | Effectiveness |
|---|---|
|  |  |
|  |  |
|  |  |
|  |  |
|  |  |

## Health note 20:

Reduce you TV Time or combine it with chores like washing dishes or sweeping.

People, who reduce their TV watching time by half, on average lose 6 kg each year.

| Day | Monday | Tuesday | Wednesday | Thursday | Friday | Saturday | Sunday |
|---|---|---|---|---|---|---|---|
| Weight | / / | / / | / / | / / | / / | / / | / / |

Daily Weight Table

## Summary:

1. Write down a list of supportive thoughts and behaviors for yourself regarding weight loss.
2. The more creative and interesting the list is, the more helpful it is in your treatment process.
3. Your list of thoughts and behaviors may not seem related to eating at first glance; however, these supportive thoughts and behaviors will increase your energy to keep going.
4. Commitment to execute these supportive behaviors is an important principle.
5. 
6. 

---

**If you want to read more**

1. Donofry SD, Stillman CM, Erickson KI. A review of the relationship between eating behavior, obesity, and functional brain network organization [published online ahead of print, 2019 Nov 4]. Soc Cogn Affect Neurosci. 2019;nsz085..

Step 21   Date:   /   /

# Automatic Eating

**How to overcome our unconscious eating?**

Have you ever finished a meal and realized you didn't notice the taste? Have you ever been so absorbed in a television show that you cleaned your plate without realizing it? Have you ever been so lost in a conversation that you suddenly realized you were stuffed?

In this step, we introduce you to another reason for overeating and being overweight which results in excessive eating. Mindless eating is the cause of being overweight in many people and is another kind of behavior that is commonly seen in obese people, meaning that you are not aware of what you are eating at the moment. For example, if you are used to having your lunch or dinner in front of the TV, you've probably eaten a meal without tasting your food. This type of eating method leads to overeating. Even when you want to be careful about your calorie intake, if you eat mindlessly, you cannot control your intake of calories. On the other hand, when people do not concentrate on eating, they do not enjoy what they are eating and they won't feel satisfied. Many other bad behavioral habits, such as fast eating, will increase in these situations. So, to modify our bad habits, we must reduce our unconscious eating.

One of the most important steps to be taken in this weight loss program is to identify these behavioral patterns and plan to reduce them. To get a better understanding of yourself, you should first get acquainted with the scientific basis of human behavior.

**Behaviors can be divided into two main categories according to their demands:**

1. Goal-driven behaviors: **When you set a new and specific goal, you must carefully and energetically adjust your behaviors to reach that goal. In the end and when you achieve the goal, you will also experience some pleasure.**

2. Stimulus-driven behaviors: **When your behaviors are based on a particular stimulus, it is often automatic and partially unconscious. You need low mental energy to perform these habitual behaviors, and you can often do so in the presence of the stimulus alone.**

Goal-driven behaviors repeated over time gradually become stimulus-driven behaviors, this is the process of learning. When you develop new skills in this way they require less energy.

**Stimulus-driven behaviors occur in three types of situations:**

1. Situations where your mental energy is low. **For example, when you come home from a hard day at work. As soon as you are exposed to foods in the fridge, you forget about your weight loss goals and start eating.**

2. Situations where you are using your energy doing something else. **For example, during a challenging business meeting, or during an important phone conversation with family members, you can't keep track of your eating behavior and eat whatever is around without realizing it.**

3. Situations where the brain is storing energy. **For example, at breakfast, you may have high mental energy, but your brain needs to keep this energy up all day long. So, it saves energy and prefers to move you towards stimulus-driven behaviors.**

Therefore, in the light of the unconscious and inattentive eating patterns mentioned, one of the most important steps to be taken in a weight loss program is to identify these patterns in yourself and plan to reduce them.

✎ Please think a little bit about your eating behavioral patterns, and see which of the following conditions increases the likelihood of your unconscious eating? Following the examples below will help you find your unconscious eating habits better.

① Eating in front of the TV.
② Eating at the desk.
③ Eating while reading a newspaper.
④ Eating when talking with colleagues at work.
⑤ Eating at the restaurant with friends.
⑥ Eating while on the phone.
⑦ Eating in the cinema.
⑧ Eating while watching football.
⑨ Eating while driving.

In addition to bad behavioral habits, like fast eating or stand-up eating that leads to unconscious eating, environmental conditions also encourage this type of eating. Like eating while watching television or discussing at the table and other causes and factors that can lead to some kind of unconscious eating in you.

With the careful engineering of our environment, we can alleviate this problem. We need to focus on the engineering of our environment once again and see what changes in the living environment can reduce our unconscious eating. Which of the following actions can work for you?

① Changing the place of TV and dining table.
② Eating on the dining table rather than in front of the TV.
③ Changing your eating places at work.
④ Eliminating newspaper reading while eating breakfast.
⑤ Eating alone at work.
⑥ Listening to music instead of watching TV while eating.

Another step you can take to reduce unconscious and mindless eating is to raise your awareness and attention to different senses while eating. For instance, look at your meal while eating and see what ingredients go into it. When you put a small bite of it in your mouth, chew it well. Touch your food with your tongue and teeth and feel the food in your mouth. Find the rigidity and smoothness of the ingredients of the food. Smell the food and feel the taste in your mouth. Pay attention to your sense which comes from the stomach. Try to stop eating based on the feeling you have from your stomach before you become full. After a while, you will surely find that if you stop eating before filling the stomach and feeling full, after a few minutes you will experience the feeling of satiety.

Performing mindfulness exercises is one of the best ways to inhibit unconscious eating. In the next step, we'll do the exercises.

In addition to mindless eating, there is another type of bad eating pattern called automatic eating, which can lead to overeating. This is when you eat without any desire or need to eat. For example, when you open the refrigerator, without a plan to eat, you take a slice of cake or an apple and eat it. When you start eating chips and you cannot stop or eat cookies mindlessly while on the phone. In automatic eating situations, it is also possible that the person is unaware and this leads to increased overeating. Automatic eating is very similar to a behavioral habit, but it is not stable. For example, if you do not have a biscuit box on your desk, you probably will not have automatic eating when you make a phone call, and won't experience the negative emotion. Remember, eating habits are well-established behaviors that are hard to change and make you feel bad if you don't do them.

Automatic eating causes hidden calorie intake into your body, calories that you may not have noticed or counted. Keep in mind that these calories are digested, consumed, and stored in our bodies, the same as when we eat consciously. Unfortunately, the pattern of automatic eating behaviors is widespread and many people who are overweight experience this.

**Think about the situations that can induce automatic eating and craving? Here are some examples.**

1. When I study for exams, I always go to the fridge.
2. During meetings, when there is a biscuit on the desk.
3. When donuts and coffee are served in the office.

One of the basic strategies to reduce automatic eating is **Environmental Engineering**. One of the most effective tactics is removing the available, high-calorie foods from the refrigerator, home, and work desks. This topic has been discussed many times in the past few steps, suggestions have been made by you and the actions you have taken so far.

In the next step of this book, we will emphasize awareness-raising methods during eating.

**Brain Box**

# What's going on in your brain?

Before reading this section, think about the following question:

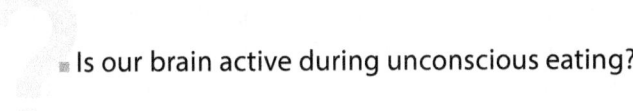

- Is our brain active during unconscious eating?

As we said earlier, the dependent brain likes to put us in certain situations. For instance, it might persuade us to go to the pastry shop and justify buying some sweets, "I'm only buying this for my friend's party." So that we do not consciously suffer if we sample a few in the shop. We might even say, "When they serve us it would be offensive not to partake." The interesting thing about the brain is that in addition to being extremely dependent, it can also be very creative and, despite your efforts to change, it will often find a way back to its routine.

In the example above, if the person decides to resist the pastry and goes to buy a house plant instead, his brain will begin working out a way to obtain the pastry, "Suppose I bought the plant and went to the party, but when I'm accepting guests, should I serve them with plants too? If I buy these sweets I don't eat them myself, I can put them on the top of the cabinet, and only take them down for guests". We know very well that most of the time before any guests come to our house, we will be tempted by the pastries and resist throwing them away. We might say, "There are hungry people. It would be wasteful for me to throw any food away." This is an example of our brain's dependence on foods. I'm sure while reading, you thought of examples from your own life. Keep these stories in mind.

In addition to dependency, the human brain can also be in an automatic state. When the brain is in automatic mode, it does well without any interference and saves a lot of energy at the same time, for example, remember the first day you learned how to drive. You didn't know where to pay attention, the rear-view mirror, the side mirrors, the steering wheel, the shifter, or, worst of all, the pedals! Let alone, the constant instruction beside you and the fear of other drivers on the road. As you get to your destination, you feel like being beaten due to the stress and you have no energy left. Imagine now, if, after several years, driving required the same amount of energy, would it make sense for our brain's limited energy to be fully spent on driving? The answer is definitely no, so our brain, through practice and repetition, gradually learns this skill to the best of its ability with the least amount of energy, so that after a few years of driving, when arriving at the destination, if you ask the person about driving, s/he may not remember anything special about it while s/he has completely obeyed all the rules. But how is the automatic brain while eating?

When the brain is in its right settings, it knows when and which network to activate, but if those settings crash, it won't work properly anymore, and for those who are overweight, their brain will eat inappropriately in an automatic state. For instance, when they are sitting in front of the TV watching their favorite series, they may eat an entire bag of chips without noticing, or one might eat a box of chocolates on the phone and not realize it! You should know that some of the situations in the living environment help the brain to stay in the automatic state. People in these situations need to learn to make adjustments manually. But how?

The brain whose settings are messed up follows a kind of stimulus-driven behavior; that is, when you see a greasy hamburger, your stimulated brain succumbs to that stimulus, so inappropriate eating occurs and the brain needs to consume a lot of energy to digest, absorb, and store fat. On the other hand, the changes and behaviors presented in this book are goal-driven. For example, if the brain is low in energy, the chance of performing goal-driven behaviors will be reduced and the brain becomes involved again with automatic behaviors i.e. stimulus-driven behaviors. For this reason, you should try to convert automatic stimulus-driven habitual behaviors into goal-driven ones by maintaining the necessary energy of the brain and making slow, step-by-step changes.

Make a list of non-eating activities and do them regularly to replace the inappropriate eating with healthy automatic behavior in situations where the brain energy is low. This list varies from person to person. One person may want to collect puzzles, while another may want to dance or study, but when your brain energy is high, plan to do environmental engineering and reduce the chance of automatic habits. For example, if you always take the train to get home at 5 pm, catch the bus this time or go for a walk to see the nearby shops. Sometimes it is a good idea to buy a small gift for yourself, as it is also a novelty for the brain.

Date: ...... / ...... / ......

## Your Own Footsteps on this Journey...

**1** Please be careful about the hidden calorie intake to your body. Identify situations that cause automatic and unnecessary eating, and write down the steps you can take to reduce or eliminate them.

| Automatic eating conditions without craving | Actions are taken to modify them |
|---|---|
| Eating nuts unconsciously while watching TV | Disposing of nuts or other foods while watching TV shows |
| Eating nuts unconsciously while watching TV | Not buying energetic nuts like walnuts and raisins |

**2** **Setting up a behavioral contract to modify automatic eating.**

A small contract for modifying eating:

I _____ Commit myself, based on the commitment and duty that I am given to my weight loss, in this week: _____

Agreement date: _____    Your signature: _____

**3** Make a list of corrective suggestions for your living environment or your daily routine so that you can eliminate automatic or less attentive eating. Rate the feasibility of these corrective suggestions from zero to one hundred.

| Suggested corrective actions to increase attention while eating | Feasibility |
| --- | --- |
|  |  |

## Health note 21:

It takes twenty minutes to send the message of satiety to the brain.
A study found that those who eat more slowly feel the satiety just as the people who eat fast, but they each receive sixty-six kilocalories less energy per serving. If you want to better understand the concept of these un-received 66 kilocalories of energy, you need to know that by slowly eating, you can lose about 20 lbs in one year.

| Day | Monday | Tuesday | Wednesday | Thursday | Friday | Saturday | Sunday |
|---|---|---|---|---|---|---|---|
| Weight | / / | / / | / / | / / | / / | / / | / / |

**Daily Weight Table**

## Summary:

1. Your brain naturally has low energy in some situations, so it drives you towards stimuli-induced behaviors.
2. Identify situations where you have low energy in your life and plan to face them.
3. Identify situations where you have high energy in life. Use this high energy to shape the goal-driven behaviors and make a difference in your life.
4. 
5. 

---

If you want to read more

1. Cohen D, Farley TA. Eating as an automatic behavior. Prev Chronic Dis. 2008;5(1):A23.
2. Cohen DA. Neurophysiological pathways to obesity: below awareness and beyond individual control. Diabetes. 2008;57(7):1768-1773. doi:10.2337/db08-0163
3. Fürtjes S, King JA, Goeke C, et al. Automatic and Controlled Processing: Implications for Eating Behavior. Nutrients. 2020;12(4):1097. Published 2020 Apr 15. doi:10.3390/nu12041097

# Step 22 Date: / /

# Mindfulness, Emotions and Eating

**How to manage overeating by having a moment to moment awareness of eating?**

"Mindfulness" in simple language means to be aware of the thoughts, behaviors, emotions, and inner feelings in all moments of life. Mindfulness is, in fact, a particular form of self-interest, in which the essential element of current presence and consciousness play a vital role in the occurrence of internal actions and reactions. In other words, keeping full and moment to moment attention, as well as having an attitude of acceptance, without any judgment about everything happening within us, is the main goal of mindfulness. A mindful person is aware of his thoughts, feelings, and behaviors when he has the desire to eat. He should be able to answer these questions in his mind:

- Why do I want to eat? (Thoughts and feelings)
- What kind of food have I chosen to eat and why?
- How much food should I prepare and eat?
- How fast do I want to eat?
- How do I feel during eating?
- How do I feel full gradually?
- When will I stop eating?
- What do I feel like shortly after eating?

Also, a mindful person is aware of his craving fluctuations, presence or absence of hunger and their ability to control cravings. A mindful person accepts the existence of these emotions and incidents within himself, without judging or feeling guilty, embarrassed, or incapacitated about their good or bad ones.

One way to manage all three kinds of eating, habitual eating, automatic eating, and craving induced eating, is to improve mindfulness. By using mindfulness methods and self-observational skill, you'll find a better understanding of satiety triggers. Achieving this skill will help you to experience satiety on time and you will not overeat. Sometimes overeating can be seen as a way to escape self-awareness, such as when you just eat to get rid of bad feelings. The mindfulness can lead to acceptance without judgment in unwelcome life situations. That is, if you are scared or angry, it will help you to accept this experience and not blame yourself for having such feelings. Every human has the right to have negative feelings without guilt, shame, or embarrassment. Mindfulness is a general skill that is used in a variety of contexts, but in this step, we will focus on application of mindfulness in managing overeating. In mindful eating, you think about the thoughts or feelings causing or accompanying eating and accept them. The idea that you would like to be alone in a candy shop so you can eat whatever you want is not an embarrassing thought. Accept this thought and feel it without judgment and carefully review its presence within yourself. You can imagine that you have put all your feelings and thoughts on a conveyor belt and they pass through your eyes, and as you consciously perceive these thoughts, you will accept that they are within yourself and at the same time you commit to change some of them over time. The more you increase your potency in mindfulness, the more you will improve.

In the following, there are several methods of mindfulness. You can improve your potency in mindfulness by learning and practicing these technics regularly.

You need to know that practicing mindfulness is like learning how to ride a bike. Initially, every effort you make fails and you may lose your balance over and over again. You may try many days without success, but eventually one day you realize that you can maintain your balance and ride a bike. Once you successfully maintain balance on a bike, then you will always be able to ride a bike. As you learn these methods, it may be hard to focus at first. You must maintain consistent training to practice mindfulness well.

**1. The imagination of clouds of thoughts:**

One of the important methods in mindfulness is visualization. In this method, you try to picture what's on your mind. To do this, follow the steps below:

- **When the eating-related thoughts come to your mind and annoy you, close your eyes and imagine writing them on a piece of paper. Be careful to write every single letter and word. Wherever the image fades, try to visualize it again and continue to write.**
- **Imagine your thoughts move on paper and slowly rise from the paper. You see a line of your writings in space.**
- **Your thoughts are moving slowly upward and surrounded by a halo of small clouds and moving upward. Try to read them in motion mode.**
- **Your thoughts clouds are still moving upward and will gradually approach the sky.**
- **The clouds of your thoughts are combined with the clouds in the sky and you cannot see them.**

Do this exercise for other thoughts. As your concentration increases, you can increase the number of thoughts written on the clouds that are moving upward. Try to perfectly visualize them, and wherever your mental image fades and your concentration drops, go back to the previous step and continue.

**2. Awareness of Craving:**

This practice can be done especially when you are having severe cravings, such as when you are heavily craving for food; for example, pasta or hamburgers. In this case, you can use this method in addition to the methods you have been trained so far.

- **Sit down somewhere, close your eyes and visualize all that is said, just as your eyes closed:**
- **First, pay attention to what goes on within you. Think of your heartbeat, the breath, the feelings you experience in your stomach, the taste of your mouth, and all that is within you.**
- **Imagine having a dish of pasta salad in front of you; describe it with closed eyes before you eat it. Think about its content, for example, you can say: This dish contains starchy pasta, greasy sausages, sweet pepper, and mayonnaise stuffed with solid oil.**
- **Go back to your inner feelings and see how you feel within yourself, in your stomach, mouth, heartbeat, and…**

- **This time, try to recall the latest movie you've seen or the most recent book you read and talk about the story of that movie or the content of the book. Try to say what you're talking about in more detail, like who was the main cast of the film, what color she was wearing, how was her makeup, which movie scene was more attractive to you and…**
- **After a few minutes, go back to your inner feelings and describe them. Has the feeling of excitement inside you been a little relaxed?**

This method helps many people to reduce their cravings because by changing your inclinations, you reduce the pressure that the craving imposes. One of the best ways to cope with craving is to reduce its strength. Using the methods of changing attention, either objectively, by performing a different task or through the awareness of inner feelings can be effective in reducing the power of craving.

Mindfulness is the core of yoga practice and meditation. Increasing people's ability to manage their attention and focusing on their inner feelings and their conscious perception makes it possible for a person to have extraordinary power in reevaluating and managing their feelings and desires, which is a very valuable power.

There is a famous Indian proverb that says: "Conquer your feelings and desires and you will conquer the world."

Mindfulness of our lives and feelings can change not only our eating habits but our entire lifestyle. Getting this valuable power cannot be done all at once, but understanding the importance of moving toward mindfulness is a positive change in your life.

**Keep in mind that,** "He who would learn to fly one day must first learn to stand and walk and run and climb and dance; one cannot fly into flying." (Friedrich Nietzsche)

### Brain Box
# What's going on in your brain?
Before reading this section, think about the following question:

- How can the brain's perception ability be changed?

The human brain interprets its environment based on external stimuli, such as the sounds in the environment, the lights, and so on, which is called perception, which means, "understanding, a taking cognizance," from Latin "perceptionem" meaning "intuitive or direct recognition of some innate quality". If a person looks inside to discover what is going on, this is called Interoception. "Intra" means inner and "ception" means to understand which constitute the interoception which is contemporarily defined as the sense of the internal state of the body. This can be both conscious and non-conscious. But what makes this interoception important?

As we discussed earlier, there is a system called "limbic" in the human brain that is not available consciously to us but has a fundamental role in generating emotions and desires. When this system is activated, it causes changes in the body that can help the person to be aware of the activity of this area.

Remember the example of pupils. One of the faces was more appealing to you. This activates the amygdala which makes your heart race, your blood pressure raise, and your skin perspire. These feelings create indirect awareness of the amygdala's activity in your brain. The greater one's inner understanding, the more aware they are about social or emotional conditions and this helps the individual to better manage his or her desires consciously. One of the ways to reinforce the interoception is meditation and mindfulness. Meditation is not a place to go but a presence, here and now. Make sure you are in a calm environment and no one is bothering you. Sit comfortably. There is no need to control the brain, breathing, or any other details. Notice where your awareness is going. Let your consciousness move freely, rather than forcibly move it to a specific place. Is there a particular feeling within you? Let your consciousness calms down and let it be as it is. When the thoughts come out, let them be the same and bring awareness back. Notice how emotions change, and consciousness naturally goes elsewhere based on inner guidance. Let awareness follow this path. It may take a while for you to work on different layers of your body and get little by little into the deeper layers. Leave the thoughts and feelings just as they are and be an observer.

During this experience and Interoception, a part of the brain called "Insula" is activated. Insula in Latin means island. As you can see in the figure, Insula (the blue area in the figure) is located under the layers of the cerebral cortex on both sides of the head and its primary function is to raise awareness as well as regulate perception and self-awareness. This area is next to the cognitive triangle of the frontal area and completes the missing piece of the "top-down" puzzle. When stimulus causes an outburst in the deep areas of the brain, we can perceive the changes through interoception and insula activity. We then reappraise this information with the help of the anterior cingulate and talk about it with the Broca's area located above the Insula.

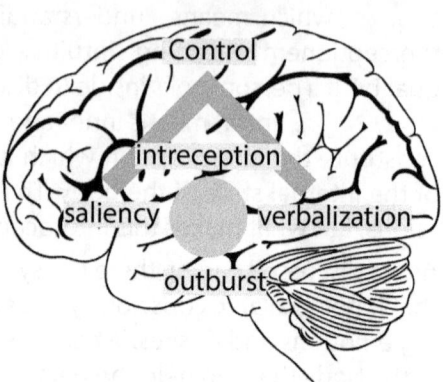

in fact, when one perceives symptoms, talks about them, and analyzes them, the brain saliency network is activated because the anterior cingulate cortex and the insula form the core of this network, and with their increased activity consciousness and awareness are also increased. The greater this awareness, the more successful craving management will be.

Date: ...... / ...... / ......

## Your Own Footsteps on this Journey...

**1** Please practice mindfulness methods until the next session, at least once a day for 15-30 minutes at home and report the results.

| Name of the method | Performing time | Results induced by this method |
|---|---|---|
| | | |
| | | |
| | | |
| | | |

**2** How can you increase your awareness while eating? Write down your suggested solutions.

## Health note 22:

Smokers think "If I quit smoking, I'll become fat." This is a false belief. Nicotine has very little effect on appetite and weight loss. The main cause of weight gain after quitting smoking is the loss of an important tool for regulating your emotions and replacing them with eating. To prevent weight gain while quitting, you need to strengthen other emotion regulation techniques.

| Day | Monday | Tuesday | Wednesday | Thursday | Friday | Saturday | Sunday |
|---|---|---|---|---|---|---|---|
|  | / / | / / | / / | / / | / / | / / | / / |
| Weight | | | | | | | |

Daily Weight Table

## Summary:

1. Our brains are capable of understanding the external environment, internal conditions, and the cognitive processes within the brain.
2. The ability to understand cognitive processes within the brain is called metacognition, and it means consciousness over consciousness.
3. Boosting metacognition and what goes on in the brain is a very valuable ability that plays a vital role in observing, describing, and ultimately managing the causes of overeating.
4. Mindfulness can be practiced daily in everyday tasks.
5. Mindfulness helps you to have a clear understanding of yourself and what you want to eat. So, it will be easier for you to ignore what is harmful to you or what you don't need.
6. 
7. 

---

If you want to read more

1. Veilleux JC, Skinner KD, Pollert GA. Examining the effect of cue exposure and introspective responses to cues on impulsivity in restrained and unrestrained eaters. Eat Behav. 2018;31:99-104. doi:10.1016/j.eatbeh.2018.09.001

Step 23    Date:    /    /

# Lapse and Relapse Prevention

One of the major concerns on the path to recovery is the recurrence of overeating behaviors. This phenomenon is seen in the early stages of recovery because the brain is still dependent and wants to go back to its original state and the individual is still unaware of the techniques to protect his treatment process. Hence, the likelihood of repeating his previous problematic behaviors is very high. But the lapse and relapse may occur at any time along the recovery path. In this step, we will address the two issues of lapse and relapse in the treatment and their differences, and the signs and symptoms of relapse, as well as actions you can take to prevent them.

First, let's get to know more about the concept of lapse and relapse. Lapse means doing the past wrong behavior after a relatively long period of avoiding that behavior. If the lapses are repeated and the person is excluded from the treatment, one might say "the disease has relapsed." The lapse is a process that begins long before overeating occurs and is completed by succumbing to overeating.

On many occasions, lapse begins with a simple everyday event, like participating in a party and not adhering to the principles of avoiding triggers and returning to past overeating behaviors. You might have heard many people who have succeeded in losing weight, fail to maintain their diets and regain their original weight.

As said, recurrence or relapse means returning to damaging behaviors and

unhealthy beliefs of the past. Relapse means complete cessation of the recovery, while the lapse is often a shortstop or stagnation in recovery. Lapse is a sign that the recovery program is not fully implemented or that the excuses and pretexts of the past remained in mind and are not eradicated. The difference between lapse and relapse is that in the lapse, the recovery process does not disappear; only its progress is stopped, while in relapse all the destructive thoughts and beliefs of the past are back in full force. A lapse can be likened to slipping, but relapse to fall. Multiple lapses or long staying in a lapse converts the lapse into relapse.

**Please review your previous experiences and think about one of the lapses that occurred to you during the last month.**

**Description of previous lapse experience:**

*Meeting old friends after a few years. We had gathered together in a restaurant and had a great time remembering youth.*

**Your reasons for lapse:**

*I've learned the way to lose weight. It's just once and it won't ruin everything.*
*I have the right to rest after some weight loss and reward myself.*
*I will be exercising more tomorrow morning.*
*I will make up tomorrow and eat much less.*
*I don't want everyone to know that I'm on a diet.*
*If I don't eat, I will ruin the gathering.*

It is important to note that lapse is part of the treatment process and a tool we can learn from because we can identify our weaknesses in the recovery path. The lapse determines what needs to be corrected or which exercise we may need to repeat.

Check the lapses in the treatment path carefully and analyze their reasons. Lapse means your treatment concepts are still not well understood. Honesty provides the opportunity for you to analyze your weaknesses by analyzing previous lapses and helping yourself to correct them.

Lapses do not happen all at once. Here are some common warning signs:

- **Lack of interest and impatience in studying and reviewing different parts of the book, not doing the exercises accurately, and not implementing book recommendations.**
- **Contact with people who you have been previously restricted your relations in**

relationship engineering, and making excuses in this area.

- **Doing things that indirectly lead to your overeating, like buying your favorite sweets or chocolates as a gift for friends when you visit them. This may indicate a person's unconscious desire for returning to overeating behaviors.**
- **Trampling the conventions and rules that help you avoid craving, such as not paying attention to environmental engineering with irrational reasoning like, I cannot ban family members from eating these foods because of my program.**
- **Disorganization, agitation, irregularities, and hanging out with food-focused friends. When you see the warning signs of lapse, you should be aware and try to fix them, because ignoring them may lead to lapse.**
- **Overworking, little fun, tiredness, and sleep deprivation that reduce your ability to inhibit the craving and increase your need for rewards and enjoyment through eating.**
- **Unwillingness to weigh regularly.**

The emerging of warning signs does not necessarily mean a relapse into overeating, but an important sign of danger for getting you closer to the past sickly overeating. In addition to warning signs, preform some activities that can be considered as preventative symptoms of relapse which strengthens you in the recovery path such as:

- **Paying attention to the warning signs of relapse and correcting them.**
- **Commitment to the principles of treatment and being patient in achieving goals.**
- **A careful study of the steps of the book.**
- **Serious attention to environment and relationship engineering.**
- **Planning, increasing regularity in life, and creating routine programs that reduce the need for day-to-day decisions.**
- **Optimal use of the frontal lobe and considering its limitations.**
- **Avoiding false diets that lead to long-term hunger.**
- **Commitment to perform Supportive Behaviors (step 20) and avoiding destructive thoughts and behaviors (step 18).**

What if we have a lapse, what can we do? The most important issue in dealing with the lapse is to understand that lapse is part of the recovery process. This helps reduce the sense of guilt and embarrassment of lapse, which is one of the important factors in relapsing. After accepting the lapse as part of the recovery process, we need to accept reality with sincerity and analyze it.

We should not care about the misconceptions of lapse such as: "A lapse means starting over", "a lapse is unavoidable, and people cannot control their weight forever", "A lapse can happen at any time", "All lapses lead to relapse", "Lapse is a sign of individual weakness," and "If a person fails he should quit" **Giving in to these falsehoods can quickly turn a lapse into a relapse.**

Of course, it should be noted that not paying attention to external factors of lapse such as irritating environments, family turmoil and stress can lead to failure of inhibition and overating will return.

Vacations and holidays are common times for a lapse to occur. Precision in the amount of energy received and regular weighing can prevent unwanted energy intakes in these situations. Increasing the level of physical activities and exercising during vacations and holidays can provide some opportunity for additional companionship with the family at the table. Keep in mind that you must not question the commands and practices described in this book, especially ignoring the contracts you have made with yourself along the way. Appreciating the beliefs and teachings of this book, even during travel, reflects your commitment to recovery.

Brain Box
## What's going on in your brain?
Before reading this section, think about the following question:

- How does the human brain find out about its processes (metacognition)?

Lapse and relapse phenomena occur over time and are part of the recovery path. No progress can be made without error. Error is the essence of the path and there are signs along with it that we must pay attention to and the prerequisite of this attention is your skill in using the techniques you have already learned, so the skills you get at the end of this path will help you adjust your treatment and move on. Another key point before lapse and relapsing is to determine an indicator that shows your adherence to treatment consistently and objectively, and if you greaten that indicator, you can stay on track. An example of these indicators is weighing that should be done daily, before breakfast, after going to the bathroom, and with minimum clothing. Whenever you feel you have no interest in weighing and are avoiding it, you should know that your movement toward failure has begun. In this section of the brain box, we will go a little further than our previous teachings and introduce the cognition of cognition, so-called metacognition. Think of the brain as an orchestra. Different brain networks, like musicians and their instruments, play different roles. The musical notes, thoughts, make up the music of our mind. Metacognition is the orchestra leader responsible for reappraisal, controlling, evaluating the processes, and awareness.

Metacognition also allows us to come out of the vortex of thoughts, feelings, and predictions and look at the things going on in our minds. Suppose something is happening in the street where you live. Father and son are arguing with each other and since the street has gotten crowded, you can't see what is happening. So, you ask a bystander about the story, and he says, "I don't know exactly what the story is, but these two guys are fighting." This answer will not satisfy you, but you cannot go further and see what is happening. Suddenly a thought comes to your mind. You go back inside, to your second-floor window, and now you are above the others. You can see what is happening more accurately and easily. Using meta-cognition is similar, instead of engaging preoccupations in your mind, you look at them from a distance and make a more specific and accurate decision about them. For example, look at a situation in which you face a trigger, an ice-cream. If you can take a step back from the situation you may remember that you ate ice-cream as a child, with your close friends in your neighborhood. While you desire this simple pleasure, what you might do instead on a hot day is take a cool shower. Now you have taken your mind off of the trigger and satisfied the root of your cravings. All of the above happens in a set of brain regions that are led by the frontal pole region. The concept of metacognition relates to other concepts such as cognitive control, such that the frontal areas based on the interaction with the insula, receive information from the body and send it to the frontal poles to enhance the cognitive and judgmental performance.

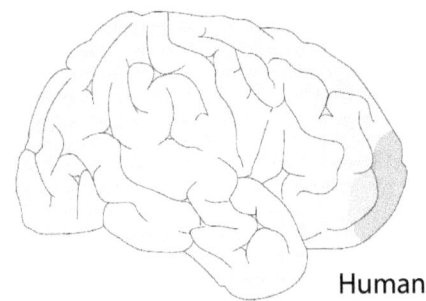

Human

Date: ...... / ...... / ......

## Your Own Footsteps on this Journey...

**1** Recall your previous two lapses and try to analyze the reasons for them based on the teachings of this book. How can you avoid the same lapses?

The first lapse

**Reason 1**

**Reason 2**

How to prevent

The second lapse

**Reason 1**

**Reason 2**

How to prevent

**2** What thoughts or behaviors are indicative of lapses? Name 5 of them.

1.
2.
3.
4.
5.

**3** What thoughts or behaviors prevent you from lapses? Name 5 of them.

1.
2.
3.
4.
5.

**4** What are the false justifications that can be a factor in your relapse and overeating in travel and holidays?

1.
2.
3.

4.

5.

**5** **What strategies can reduce the likelihood of relapse and overeating during trips and holidays?**

1.

2.

3.

4.

5.

**6** **In the case of relapse and overeating for a few days, how will you return to the recovery path?**

1.

2.

3.

4.

5.

## Health note 23:

Do you need to buy sweets, chocolates, or caramels to give as gifts to others?
Even when you decide to go to a bakery and buy a gift for one of your friends, be sure to answer this question before you buy it: Are you really buying this for your friends or for yourself?

| Day | Monday | Tuesday | Wednesday | Thursday | Friday | Saturday | Sunday |
|---|---|---|---|---|---|---|---|
| Weight | / / | / / | / / | / / | / / | / / | / / |

**Daily Weight Table**

## Summary:

1. Accept relapse as part of the recovery process and don't feel guilty about it as much as possible.
2. Try not to create a sweet and enjoyable memory through relapse. Such memories may keep you away from the recovery process.
3. If the relapses are analyzed in a written mode and their reasons are reviewed, they will provide valuable information about yourself which will guide you on the path to recovery.
4. Relapses do not occur without precursors and alarms. Heed these warnings and take them seriously.
5. Reduce exposure to triggers as much as possible to prevent lapses.
6. 
7. 

---

If you want to read more

1. Olstad S, Solem S, Hjemdal O, Hagen R. Metacognition in eating disorders: comparison of women with eating disorders, self-reported history of eating disorders or psychiatric problems, and healthy controls. Eat Behav. 2015;16:17-22. doi:10.1016/j.eatbeh.2014.10.019

Step 24   Date:    /    /

# Conscious Eating and Mindful Emotions
**I'm happy, aware, and committed to change!**

So far, you've learned a lot about eating behavior. You know that not every eating behavior is natural and correct. Many eating behaviors are without a real need and may be induced by improper habits, automatic eating, or cravings. You will no longer be able to act as you did without knowing the reason for your overeating. Even if you are overeating, you know what is the cause of this inappropriate behavior. This awareness ultimately prevents you from experiencing overeating like before. You will no longer be at disposal of triggers surrounding you to induce a disabling craving.

New knowledge will give you a fresh attitude over time and your behavior will change as a result of it. You can empower yourself in controlling eating by learning new information and doing the exercises of previous steps. Do not forget what keeps you safe from being overweight is completing a course of treatment, and doing its exercises regularly. You may still sometimes tend to overeat. It's best to think about the reason and the possible causes of it. One of the reasons may be not doing or following the exercises of previous steps.

✎ If the desire to overeat has been emerged again, answer the following five questions:

1. **What happened before this feeling?**
2. **When does this tendency to overeat happen usually?**
3. **Does this tendency occur in the presence of a particular person?**
4. **Does it happen in a particular location?**
5. **Is there a tendency for a particular food?**

By answering these questions, you can analyze the cause of your desire and find out if there was something you did not pay attention to during various exercises or maybe you haven't fully understood the previous exercises? Once you have diagnosed your problem, please read the related step again and repeat its exercises.

As mentioned in the previous steps, one of the successful tools of managing your overeating is your ability to modify the surrounding environment and relationships. For example, imagine a mother who has to cook high-calorie greasy foods due to the pressure of her children and husband, without having the possibility to go to the gym and exercise to burn the extra calories like they do. In this situation, all family members expect her to accompany them at lunch or dinner. It is clear that in these conditions, despite the all triggers and craving induced from them, our work to lose weight will be difficult. Some people in this situation think that nothing can be done to solve this problem, and so they "suffer in silence." Although this is a complicated problem, it certainly has solutions. Surely the solution to this problem is not the arguments and fights within the family. Our experience shows that most people who have such problems in their family, by being patient, clever planning, talking with family, and getting help from influential people can be successful in engineering the environment and relationships over time without causing a family issue.

Another reason for continued overeating is not being happy. As mentioned earlier in the previous steps, one important action in your treatment is paying attention to the recreational activities and pleasures other than eating. Because our mental system requires regular rewards and a variety of activities other than eating to help us earn this reward. Now that you are aware of your weight, you care about your happiness and you know that worrying about weight only increases your problem. Consider yourself, "A happy, and self- aware person." From this state, you may become permanently mindful and bring yourself to an ideal weight. Be sure that the rate at which you lose weight reflects your awareness of all the training provided in this book.

Fast weight change is not necessarily a good sign. If you lose weight without modifying your environment and your thoughts in a short period with high pressures on your own, you will lose weight at high speed but maintaining this weight loss will be difficult.

Maintaining proper balance and speed are the main teachings of this book. What is essential for your success after a joyful consciousness is your commitment to change. Knowledge alone does not necessarily mean change. You must also prove your commitment to change. Commitment is aligned with the associated costs. Costs can include time, energy, or money. Someone who is aware of the problem and has also learned how to solve it. If he does not pay the cost, he will be unable to make the change and solve the problem. The following can indicate that you are committed to solving your problem:

- **Study and review previous discussions in each step over time.**
- **Doing exercises think deeply about the teachings of the book.**
- **Weighing and recording weight regularly in this booklet.**
- **Getting help from experts to implement the book's teachings if needed.**
- **Considering the time and performing activities that keep you on the path of recovery and make you a step forward and avoid destructive activities.**
- **Buying low-calorie foods and avoid purchasing high-calorie ones, even if they are tasty or cheap.**
- **Continuing the path of the book's teachings even after completing its study.**

All these activities are for reform. You need to create new memories, recreational activities, and ultimately new thoughts and beliefs in your life to keep up with these changes you have made. Having fun without eating, enjoyable memories with healthy, non-eating activities will gradually change your beliefs and attitude towards eating behavior.

Another important point is that if you have chosen self-awareness and health as an important value in your life, you will never reach the end of the path. You may achieve a specific goal, but living on that value will create new goals all the time so that your health goals become a lifelong journey.

If you've been able to create the three features of awareness, happiness, and commitment to change during the study of this book, we have succeeded in achieving our goal.

✎ **Think about the changes you have made during this period and what you have learned about yourself. Think about your weaknesses and see what parts of this book you should work on. Here are some examples.**

1. I feel good about myself and I think I've changed a lot. I know myself better. I have to work more on environmental engineering.
2. My relationship with my family and those around me has improved. I feel like I've been able to find myself and build a better relationship with others. But I'm still having trouble in reappraising the craving.
3. I feel like I've defeated an old giant. I feel like a hero. But I lapse sometimes.
4. I have lost 30 pounds without regrets. But I still have habitual eating.
5. I have thoroughly changed my life and discovered new fun activities to enjoy more. I'm still weak in controlling my craving.
6. I've discovered the feeling of satiety in myself. I could never feel when I was full. Mindfulness has helped me a lot, but I'm still weak in managing my relationships.
7. 

✎ **What are your suggestions for continuing the recovery path after reading this book? Pay attention to the examples people mentioned as their goals.**

1. Making sports an integral part of my life.
2. Encouraging my family to read books, watch movies, and think about themselves.
3. Reading the book again and think more about myself.
4. Deepen my connection with my new friends I have found in the sports club.
5. Actively looking for places in my city to have fun and sharing it with others.
6.

### Brain Box
# What's going on in your brain?

Before reading this section, think about the following questions:

- Try to recall all the information you have learned so far about the brain and eating.
- How do triggers get into your brain? What ultimately determines whether or not you give in?

Humans naturally move toward pleasure, and pleasure is associated with dependence. The healthy dependence we have regarding our partner, children, and friends is what keeps us going, but it's our unhealthy dependencies that make the problem.

The brain depends on reward; a reward that is a combination of pleasure and relaxation, and any phenomenon associated with reward, in the next step, create pleasure and relaxation in the brain so that when we enjoy something we try to repeat, and with each repetition, learning happens and a new memory is created in regard to it. As such, our values are formed based on it, and gradually we see a phenomenon on which we become increasingly dependent, and sometimes our dependence on the brain becomes malignant.

Suppose you go on a trip next week and get to know new food and fall in love with its taste and smell. Your brain's reward circuits are activated and you experience pleasure, and there is a surge in your deep unconsciousness so that you may want to eat it for several days or even get the recipe to prepare it when you return home. With each experience of eating this food, your brain communicates between triggers and the experience of pleasure, and a memory is created; an emotional memory that becomes stronger day by day.

In this situation, when you see the food, your brain begins to develop a spurious need to eat it because of its dependency and does not pay attention to other foods in the environment. Then processes in the brain begin to evaluate the nutrient value and importance of it. On the other hand, memories play a vital role in showing off its importance and affirming the eating of that food. Eventually, the person starts craving and the struggle between the deep and frontal areas of the brain begins and potency of the brain determines the victor.

The process is illustrated below. Try to describe each section based on the teachings of the previous steps in your language, and the techniques you use to manage them, as well as the brain regions and networks, involved. For example, in the attention section, by seeing triggers, the limbic system and attention network (top-down) activate, the individual won't see other stimuli in the environment, and the deep areas do their best to achieve pleasure, but by environmental engineering techniques, the triggers can be removed from the environment and reduce the sensitivity of the attentional network, or by behavior activation, provide the non-eating recreation activities for the pleasure of the limbic system.

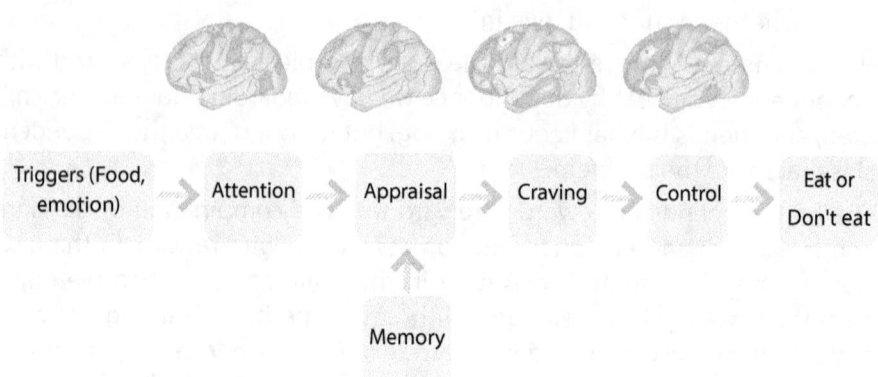

Date: ...... / ...... / ......

## Your Own Footsteps on this Journey...

**1  Please write in the lines below: what important things you have learned in this book:**

 

**2  Which step was more interesting for you?**

**3** **Which section or sections and what exercises were difficult for you?**

**4** **In your opinion, what topics should be allocated with more steps?**

**5** **Please set the following contracts to fix your treatment.**

> A small contract for the implementation of the book's teachings after its termination:
>
> I           Commit myself, based on the commitment and duty that I am given to my weight loss, After completing the study of this book:
>
> 
>
> Agreement date:                    Your signature:

> Small contract to strengthen environmental engineering:
>
> I           Commit myself, based on the commitment and duty that I am given to my weight loss, After completing the study of this book:
>
> 
>
> Agreement date:                    Your signature:

> A small contract for recreational activities with mobility and without eating:
>
>  I _____ Commit myself, based on the commitment and duty that I am given to my weight loss, After completing the study of this book:
>
> _____
>
> Agreement date: _____    Your signature: _____

## Last talk:

If you are reading this page of the book, congratulations to you! You have patiently and sincerely taken the recovery path with us which may be new to many, especially in a society that is always looking for the fastest and easiest way to reach its destination and to achieve the ideal weight. In this condition, unfortunately, the profiteers start to deceive ordinary people by false advertising like the magical weight loss pills or vibration machines for weight loss or the calorie-burning smoothies and thousands of other ways of harming your health.

We are not looking at people's attitude toward these paths, but our main goal in each of the past 24 steps has been to talk about something important, fundamental, effective, and powerful; a phenomenon that you may have heard of -The intelligent brain- by the help of which we have tried to take small but continuous steps to bring about great change and we hope that the knowledge within this book act as a light to illuminate the path of many who seek to change their lifestyles and have a new look. Maybe it is time to start from yourself, do not accept anything easily, and don't follow the advice of those around you blindly. Before making any changes, study its scientific background, consider other approaches, and choose what's best for you. The time to accept any weight loss fad is over. The knowledge of what is true is your right!

**Please read these last few lines several times:**

You may know many others who fall into the trap of fraudulent weight-loss fads and systems. They are blinded by the rigid and erroneous societal standards of beauty, self-esteem, and fake information. By the time they become aware, they have already damaged their health. Think of them before it is too late. This book may just open a new door for them as it has for you.

## Health note 24:

Absolute vegetarianism and the removal of animal proteins is not our recommended option for weight loss.

| Day | Monday | Tuesday | Wednesday | Thursday | Friday | Saturday | Sunday |
|---|---|---|---|---|---|---|---|
| Weight | / / | / / | / / | / / | / / | / / | / / |

**Daily Weight Table**

## Summary:

1. The end of this book is the beginning of conscious life. Self-knowledge has no end, with constant effort, study, and follow-up, you can gain a better understanding of yourself.

2. To be happy, you need to plan and actively change your lifestyle so that you feel good. Don't wait for a good feeling to come. Changing your behaviors will make you feel good.

3. Be committed to maintaining the changes you have made over the years, and most important is keeping your body and brain healthy. This commitment will bring you a healthy and productive life.

4.

5.

---

If you want to read more

1. Onaolapo, A. Y., & Onaolapo, O. J. (2018). Food additives, food and the concept of 'food addiction': is stimulation of the brain reward circuit by food sufficient to trigger addiction?. Pathophysiology, 25(4), 263-276.

2. Joranby, L., Pineda, K. F., & Gold, M. S. (2005). Addiction to food and brain reward systems. Sexual Addiction & Compulsivity, 12(2-3), 201-217.

# Summary in ten steps

We are very pleased that you have come along with this 24-step path and have learned the lessons of this book. At the end of the book, we will attempt to highlight some important points in the final pages that have been less discussed within the steps.

**1. Is it necessary to be careful about the nutritional values available in a variety of foods and the accumulation and multiplication of the amount of energy taken during the day to lose weight?**

To answer this question, we will draw your attention to the behavior of people around who have normal weight. Do they regularly calculate the number of calories they enter into their body and are constantly worried about how to burn 100 kilos of calories? The fact is that our emphasis in this book is on changing the environment, attitudes and thoughts about eating, intending to become a natural, non-dependent, happy and healthy person. Nutrition Knowledge about calories of different foods is good till it doesn't make you worried and anxious and it is not necessary for losing weight. If you want to constantly add and subtract the calories, the concern with this knowledge may be destructive. So, our advice is to replace some of the following general recommendations instead of a frequent reading of nutrition books to calculate the calories of foods:

**A.** The consumption of fresh fruits and vegetables throughout the day is necessary and unlimited. Only high-calorie fruits such as bananas, melons, or grapes should be consumed more carefully. Cucumber, apple and pomegranate are heavenly fruits.

**B.** Urban people today do not need to get high amounts of starch from rice, bread or pasta, so reduce them as much as possible in your daily diet.

**C.** Regular or diet soda pop and even a variety of flavored soft beer, contain high levels of sugar which increase our appetite. Instead, water is the healthiest and most refreshing drink while eating meals.

**2. Is it necessary to keep a diet for losing weight?**

Any restrictions on your nutrition should be substantial, applicable in the long term and easy. Change your eating habits and types of consumed food in a way, which makes you feel better. Learn a variety of new ways to create different salads, prepare healthy foods on Sunday for other days of the week, like cooking chicken breast, grilling fish or washing and chopping broccoli and carrots, so when you get back home tired and hungry from work, instead of making fatty scrambled egg, there is a healthy, low-calorie but delicious food in the refrigerator.

### 3. In our culture, overeating and obesity have not been a negative phenomenon. Can these conditions lead to more obesity in society?

In our culture, in many cases, people with overweight are described by words such as chubby, this is while the equivalents of this term (fat) generally are considered more negative. These cultural conditions make many overweight people, especially men, feel less upset and guilty and think about losing weight. Does increasing the negative burden associated with obesity improve the conditions in our country? The answer to this question is complicated. Studies show that if you increase the negative burden of obesity, even though more people are thinking of weight loss, the success rate for weight loss decreases. The evidence of this incident is that there are many cases of extreme obesity in western societies. Therefore, having a sense of guilt, helplessness, and depression, associated with being overweight, reduces the hope to succeed in losing weight. Our suggestion is to emphasize the concept of "commitment to change."

### 4. What is the role of exercise in weight loss?

Exercising is one of the first things that come to mind for people who seek to lose weight. But in many of these people, exercise does not affect weight loss and is discontinued after a while. Why? Before exercising, during the weight loss program, we need to determine our goals of exercise; that is, what long-term results can exercise brings us, and what results are not obtained from exercise. We also need to know how and what sport to do, which can be continued in the long-term.

### 5. If a medical specialist detects a specific disease, such as diabetes or fatty liver, and prohibits me from overeating, will it increase my weight loss probability?

Our experience in all these years suggests that about one-third of people who get a doctor's advice to lose weight can somewhat inhibit their overeating. But most people, although having gotten these recommendations and increased their efforts to control eating, are not successful in weight loss. Some people can even become overweight after this medical advice! Let's review the teachings of this book together. Long-term craving inhibition will not succeed. If the emotional and environmental triggers do not decrease, and our thoughts do not modify in analyzing them, even a very strong motivation, without learning the correct way to manage overeating, will eventually not be a success. So, if for any reason you have this strong motivation to lose weight, use this force in the right place to be effective.

### 6. How effective are other non-dietary methods, such as surgery, in losing weight?

So far, various interventions such as a balloon, gastric band or even partial removal of intestines have been suggested for weight loss through surgery. These methods have a relatively acceptable weight loss effect for at least an intermediate-term, but their long-term effects and their potential risks are very serious in the short term. The world's top medical authorities recommend using these methods to a limited group of obese people. The terms and conditions of this recommendation are being severely obese (weighing over one hundred and thirty-four kilograms for tall people) and not being successful in six months of psychological treatment of obesity with the presence of expert therapists. These methods are not advisable before attempting and experiencing psychological interventions under the supervision of a therapist or teachings of this book.

### 7. Are there times during the overweight management period, when you can have a day off and return to your overeating? For example, during travel, or special occasions, such as Christmas.

The ultimate goal of cognitive interventions is to reduce your overeating, engineering the environment and changing your thoughts and behaviors, in such a way that overeating wouldn't be your choice in everyday routine. In this ideal situation, even in travels or parties, even though your calorie intake may be slightly increased by consuming some of the healthy foods, your behavioral skills will prevent you from continuing to overeat and they will manage your extra calorie intake by exercising or reducing calorie intake in the next few days. Accordingly, "having a day off" is not an accepted concept in cognitive-behavioral interventions of obesity. Having a day off means that you are behaving as a result of an external or internal pressure without any desire or acceptance, while our ideal goal is changing you in a way that choosing healthy eating behaviors would be done consciously with internal satisfaction.

**8. Is the presence of a therapist, and regular participation at therapeutic sessions, necessary for success in cognitive-behavioral methods?**

Reading this book, doing its exercises and thinking about its teachings can be an important step to reach the ideal cognitive conditions for managing your overeating. Many people use this book separately as a tool for managing their overeating. However, for people who are more seriously intent on weight loss, and cognitive change over a given period, the presence of a therapist and regular attendance at the treatment sessions is generally helpful. About a year before the book was published, around 100 doctors, psychologists and nutritionists from all over the country served as therapists to implement the cognitive-behavioral interventions of this book in the form of an IPOM (Integrative Package for Overeating and Management) and this network of therapists is being promoted.

**9. When will the Effectiveness of Cognitive Behavioral Therapy for obesity start?**

Cognitive-behavioral therapy courses for obesity are generally held in twenty-four sessions within six months as weekly meetings for about one and a half hours. An important question among clients is, "How is the weight loss process during the course of treatment?" In response, it should be noted that the onset of weight loss varies among clients. Some people from the very first session begin to lose weight, and others will not be able to make a serious change in their weight before the first three months. Some people even gain weight for a few weeks to get a better understanding of their internal features. The level of treatment effectiveness should go beyond certain limits to begin to lose weight. This certain limit or threshold level varies from person to person, sometimes it comes with a therapeutic session and sometimes it requires several successive sessions. But the interesting point about the effectiveness of this kind of change in cognition and behavior is the length of the effect of this method. The effects of these interventions will generally accompany the client to the end of his life. Interestingly, some people have reached the threshold level after the end of the course and begin to lose weight and follow its path to the end of life. This kind of effectiveness schedule can also be correct for the teachings of this book.

**10.** **What is the most important core of success in reducing overeating through cognition?**

In our opinion, "commitment to change" is the most important part of your success in managing to overeat. Once you have modified the position of overweight and overeating in the value system of life, then you can take the first step for change, which is accompanied by acceptance without judging the problem. Having persistence and continuing to move in the direction of change, financial and time investment in order to achieve new values in life, altogether will express the level of your commitment and success on this path.

www.ingramcontent.com/pod-product-compliance
Lightning Source LLC
LaVergne TN
LVHW021601070426
835507LV00015B/1892